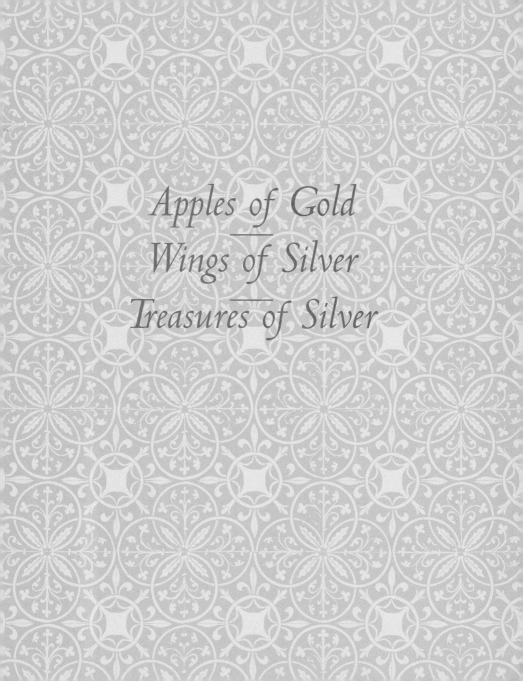

Apples of Gold

Wings of Silver

Treasures of Silver

Apples of Gold
Wings of Silver
Treasures of Silver

THE GREATEST WORKS OF
Jo Petty

First Inspirational Press edition published in 1998.

Inspirational Press
A division of BBS Publishing Corporation
386 Park Avenue South
New York, NY 10016

Inspirational Press is a registered trademark of BBS Publishing Corporation.

Published by arrangement with The C. R. Gibson Company, Norwalk, Connecticut.

Library of Congress Catalog Card Number: 98-75384

ISBN: 0-88486-218-6

Printed in the United States of America.

Contents

APPLES OF GOLD

LOVE • JOY • PEACE
LONG SUFFERING
GENTLENESS • GOODNESS
FAITH • MEEKNESS • TEMPERANCE

LOVE

Scientists know only what love does.
Love, properly applied, could virtually empty our asylums,
our prisons, our hospitals.
Love is the touchstone of psychiatric treatment.
Love can be fostered, extended, used to subjugate hate
and thus cure diseases. More and more clearly every day, out of
biology, anthropology, sociology, history, economics, psychology,
the plain common sense, the necessary mandate of survival—
that we love our neighbors as ourselves—is being confirmed
and reaffirmed. Christ gave us only one commandment—Love . . .
Now to the laboratory with love!

To love is virtually to know; to know is not virtually to love.

Real friends are those who, when you've made a fool of yourself,
don't feel that you've done a permanent job.

Work is love made visible.

It also takes two to make up after a quarrel.

Faults are thick when love is thin.

To love life through labor is to be intimate
with life's inmost secret.

Do not judge your friend until you stand in his place.

He who sows courtesy reaps friendship,
and he who plants kindness gathers love.

You shall judge a man by his foes as well as by his friends.

Adolescence is the age at which children stop asking questions
because they know all the answers.

Except in occasional emergencies there is not much
that one man can do for another,
other than to help him to help himself.

The door to the human heart can be opened only from the inside.

Friendship is to be purchased only by friendship.

Let us be the first to give a friendly sign, to nod first, smile first,
speak first, and—if such a thing is necessary—forgive first.

The light of friendship is like the light of phosphorus,
seen all around is dark.

I did a favor yesterday,
A kindly little deed . . .
And then I called to all the world
To stop and look and heed.
They stopped and looked and flattered me
In words I could not trust,
And when the world had gone away
My good deed turned to dust.

A very tiny courtesy
I found to do today;
'Twas quickly done, with none to see,
And then I ran away . . .
But someone must have witnessed it,
For—truly I declare—
As I sped back the stony path
Roses were blooming there!

Restraint without love is barbarity.
Love without restraint commits suicide.

For we must share if we would keep
That blessing from above;
Ceasing to give, we cease to have,
Such is the law of love.

If a single man achieves the highest kind of love, it will be sufficient
to neutralize the hate of millions.

Love cannot be wasted. It makes no difference where it is bestowed,
it always brings in big returns.

God pardons like a mother, who kisses the offense
into everlasting forgetfulness.

To handle yourself, use your head;
To handle others, use your heart.

Measure your life by loss instead of gain; not by the wine drunk,
but in the wine poured forth, for love's strength stands in love's
sacrifice; and who suffers most has most to give.

The only safe and sure way to destroy an enemy
is to make him your friend.

Are you lonely, O my brother?
Share your little with another!
Stretch a hand to one unfriended,
And your loneliness is ended.

The only greatness is unselfish love.

Return to him who does you wrong your purest love,
and he will cease from doing wrong;
for love will purify the heart of him who is beloved as truly as it
purifies the heart of him who loves.

Creation of woman from the rib of man: She was not made of his
head to top him; nor out of his feet to be trampled upon by him;
but out of his side to be equal with him;
under his arm to be protected; and near his heart
to be beloved.

A foreigner is a friend I haven't met yet.

The only way to have a friend is to be one.

It is only the forgiving who are qualified to receive forgiveness.

The father is the head of the house—
The mother is the heart of the house.

The love you liberate in your work is the love you keep.

How seldom we weigh our neighbor in the same balance
with ourselves.

A friend is a person with whom you dare to be yourself.

Add all the love of all the parents
and the total sum cannot be multiplied enough times to express
God's love for me, the least of His children.

A long life is barely enough for a man and a woman
to understand each other; and to be understood is to love.
The man who understands one woman is qualified to understand
pretty well everything.

Not the quarry, but the chase,
Not the trophy but the race.

Love is not soft like water, it is hard like rock, on which the waves
of hatred beat in vain.

It is in loving, not in being loved, the heart is blessed; it is
in giving, not in seeking gifts, we find our quest; whatever be
your longing or your need, that give; so shall your soul be fed,
and you indeed shall live.

To learn and never be filled is wisdom;
To teach and never be weary is love.

Conscience is God's presence in man.

Mrs.—Do you love me still?
Mr.—Yes, better than any other way.

God regards the greatness of the love that prompts the man,
rather than the greatness of his achievement.

It is absurd to pretend that one cannot love the same woman always
as to pretend that a good artist needs several violins
to play a piece of music.

I married her because we have so many faults in common.

We like someone because. We love someone although.

A friend is one who knows all about you and still likes you.

Go often to the house of your friend,
for weeds choke up the unused path.

Your friend has a friend, and your friend's friend has a friend;
be discreet.

He that cannot forgive others breaks the bridge over which
he must pass, for every man has need to be forgiven.

To understand is to pardon.

Friendship is the only cement that will ever hold the world together.

Always forgive your enemies, nothing annoys them so much.

Love is the passionate and abiding desire on the part of two
or more people to produce together conditions under which
each can be, and spontaneously express, his real self; to produce
together an intellectual soil and an emotional climate in which each
can flourish, far superior to what either could achieve alone.

The best way for a husband to clinch an argument
is to take her in his arms.

The bonds of matrimony aren't worth much
unless the interest is kept up.

One reason why a dog is such a lovable creature
is that his tail wags instead of his tongue.

Come what may, hold fast to love! Though men should rend
your heart, let them not embitter or harden it. We win
by tenderness; we conquer by forgiveness.

One of the mysteries of life is how the boy who
wasn't good enough to marry the daughter can be the father
of the smartest grandchild in the world.

Friends are made by many acts—and lost by only one.

Pure religion is love in action.

The smallest good deed is better than the grandest intention.

I've found a little remedy
To ease the life we live
And make each day a happier one—
It is the word "forgive."

So often little things come up
That leave a pain and sting,
That covered up at once would not
Amount to anything.

'Tis when we hold them up to view,
And brood and sulk and fret,
They greater grow before our eyes;
'Twere better to forget.

Politeness is a small price to pay for the good will
and affection of others.

The greater the man, the greater the courtesy.

The coin of God's realm is love.

A partnership with God is motherhood.

It is better to have loved and lost than never to have loved at all.

American Creed: Patriotism that leaps over the fence of party prejudice. Religion that jumps over the wall of intolerance. Brotherhood that climbs over the mountain of national separations.

The best gifts are tied with heartstrings.

Man is probably the only animal that even attempts to have anything to do with his half-grown young.

Every calling is great when greatly pursued.

An injurious truth has no merit over an injurious lie.

A friend is one who comes to you when all others leave.

He drew a circle that shut me out,
But love and I had the wit to win;
We drew a larger circle that took him in.

Mothers, as well as fools, sometimes walk where angels fear to tread.

When a man does a noble act, date him from that. Forget his faults. Let his noble act be the standpoint from which you regard him.

A mistake at least proves somebody stopped talking long enough to do something.

A teacher affects eternity; he can never tell where his influence stops.

'Twas her thinking of others made you think of her.

Water that is distant is no good for a fire that is near.

Success in marriage is much more than finding the right person; it is a matter of being the right person.

Hate is a prolonged manner of suicide.

Some women work so hard to make good husbands that they never quite manage to make good wives.

Put yourself in his place.

What counts is not the number of hours you put in, but how much you put in the hours.

Love sees through a telescope—not a microscope.

Some people give and forgive; others get and forget.

He makes no friends who never made a foe.

If you had to do it over, would you fall in love
with yourself again?

Ceremonies are different in every country, but trues politeness
is everywhere the same.

JOY

There is nothing I can give you that you have not, but there
is much that while I cannot give you, you can take: No heaven
can come to us unless our hearts find rest in it today. Take Heaven.
No peace lies in the future that is not hidden in this present instant.
Take Peace. The gloom of the world is but a shadow; behind it,
yet within reach, is joy. Take Joy.

It is easy to be pleasant
When life flows by like a song,
But the man worthwhile is one who will smile,
When everything goes dead wrong.

For the test of the heart is trouble,
And it always comes with the years,
And the smile that is worth the praises of earth
Is the smile that shines thru the tears.

Keep your enthusiasms, and forget your birthdays—formula for youth!

Do you see difficulties in every opportunity
or opportunities in every difficulty?

If you would know the greatest sum in addition, count your blessings.

I can alter my life by altering my attitude of mind.

As torrents in summer, half dried in their channels,
Suddenly rise, 'tho the sky is still cloudless,
For rain has been falling far off at their fountains:
So hearts that are fainting grow full to o'erflowing,
And they that behold it marvel, and know not
That God at their fountains, so far off has been raining.

Happiness is possible only when one is busy. The body must toil,
the mind must be occupied, and the heart must be satisfied.
Those who do good as opportunity offers are sowing seed all the time,
and they need not doubt the harvest.

Joy, temperance, and repose
Slam the door on the doctor's nose.

One of the great arts of living is the art of forgetting.

He who would have nothing to do with thorns
must never attempt to gather flowers.

Don't let the seeds spoil your enjoyment of a watermelon.
Just spit out the seeds.

Little and often fills the purse.

You grow up the day you have your first real laugh—
at yourself.

There is no place more delightful than one's own fireside.

When shall we all learn that the good news needs the telling,
and that all men need to know?

Keep on your toes and you won't run down at the heels.

Interesting people are people who are interested.
Bores are people who are bored.

Yes, it's pretty hard, the optimistic old woman admitted. I have to get
along with only two teeth—one upper, one lower—
but, thank goodness, they meet.

Some cause happiness wherever they go;
others whenever they go.

Happiness is a perfume you cannot pour on others
without getting a few drops on yourself.

I'm so glad I'm back home, I'm glad I went.

I do not feel any age yet. There is no age to the spirit.

To what avail the plow or sail, or land, or life, if freedom fail?

To be without some of the things you want
is an indispensable part of happiness.

There are no uninteresting things, there are only
uninteresting people.

I want a soul so full of joy—
Life's withering storms cannot destroy.

Diner: "Do you serve crabs here?"
Waiter: "We serve anyone; sit down."

The worse bankrupt in the world is the man who has lost
his enthusiasm. Let him lose everything but enthusiasm
and he will come through again to success.

I have noticed that folks are generally about as happy
as they have made up their minds to be.

If you want to be happy,
Begin where you are,
Don't wait for some rapture
That's future and far.

Begin to be joyous, begin to be glad
And soon you'll forget
That you ever were sad.

Two tragedies in life: One is not to get your heart's desire.
The other is to get it.

For all its terrors and tragedies . . . the life of man is a thing
of potential beauty and dignity . . . To live is good.

I know what happiness is, for I have done good work.

Growing old is no more than a bad habit which a busy person
has no time to form.

The only consistently bright life is the persistently right life.

What one has, one ought to use; and whatever he does
he should do with all his might.

One day as I sat musing
Alone and melancholy and without a friend,
There came a voice from out of the gloom,
Saying, "Cheer up! Things might be worse."
So I cheered up,
And sure enough—things got worse.

God does not deduct from man's allotted time
those hours spent in fishing.

An unfailing mark of a blockhead is the chip on his shoulder.

Keep ascending the mountain of cheerfulness by daily
scattering seeds of kindness along the way as best you can,
and, should mists hide the mountaintop, continue undaunted
and you will reach the sun-tipped heights
in your own life-experience.

Let us realize that what happens around us is largely
outside our control, but the way we choose to react to it
is inside our control.

The only way on earth to multiply happiness is to divide it.

How many smiles from day to day
I've missed along my narrow way!
How many kindly words I've lost
What joy has my indifference cost!
This glorious friend that now I know
Would have been friendly years ago.

It is not he who has little, but he who wants more,
who is poor.

A man's mind is like his car. If it gets to knocking too much, he'd better have it overhauled or change it.

Never miss an opportunity to make others happy, even if you have to let them alone to do it.

Old age isn't so bad . . . when you consider the alternative.

The really happy man is the one who can enjoy the scenery when he has to take a detour.

Success is a bright sun that obscures and makes ridiculously unimportant all the little shadowy flecks of failure.

The cost of a thing is that amount of life that must be exchanged for it.

Mirth is from God, and dullness is from the devil. You can never be too sprightly, you can never be too good-tempered.

Plan your work—work your plan.

Change yourself and your work will seem different.

Be cheerful. Of all things you wear, your expression is the most important.

To be happy ourselves is a most effectual contribution
to the happiness of others.

I am born happy every morning.

So long as enthusiasm lasts, so long is youth still with us.

Apart from enthusiasm, joy cannot live.

The world belongs to the enthusiast who keeps cool.

Be a lamp in the chamber if you cannot be a star in the sky.

What sunshine is to flowers, smiles are to humanity.

If we fill our hours with regrets over the failures of yesterday,
and with worries over the problems of tomorrow,
we have today in which to be thankful.

Blessed is the man who digs a well from which
another may draw faith.

Spilled on this earth are all the joys of heaven.

The secret of being miserable is to have the leisure to bother
about whether you are happy or not.

Always speak the truth and you'll never be concerned
with your memory.

There is no duty we so much underrate as the duty of being happy.

Just think how happy you'd be if you lost everything you have right
now—and then got it back again.

Earth is crammed with heaven
And every common bush is afire with God.

Remember that the coin you clutch has never brought happiness.
The world and you will profit more from sincere thoughtfulness.

They told him it couldn't be done.
With a smile, he went right to it.
He tackled the thing that couldn't be done
And couldn't do it.

May you live all the days of your life.

When a man has a "pet peeve" it's remarkable how often he pets it.

The real democratic American idea is not that every man shall be on
a level with every other, but that every man shall have liberty,
without hindrance, to be what God made him.

He who receives a benefit with gratitude repays
the first installment on his debt.

If I keep a green bough in my heart, the singing bird will come.

You have no more right to consume happiness without producing it
than to consume wealth without producing it.

Cold and reserved natures should remember
that, though not infrequently flowers may be found
beneath the snow, it is chilly work to dig for them
and few care to take the trouble.

Every man's work is a portrait of himself.

Economy makes happy homes and sound nations; instill it deep.

Things are pretty well evened up in this world. Other people's
troubles are not so bad as yours, but their children are a lot worse.

The office of government is not to confer happiness, but to give men
the opportunity to work out happiness for themselves.

If you would make a man happy, do not add to his possessions
but subtract from the sum of his desires.

Why help to make the work a dreary place—
Why be a rainy day?
Why harp on old mistakes that we regret?
Why be a rainy day?
Why wear a dismal mask of hopelessness?
Why be a rainy day?

Sorrow with his pick mines the heart, but he is a cunning
workman. He deepens the channels whereby happiness may enter,
and he hollows out new chambers for joy to abide in,
when he is gone.

Children are a great comfort in your old age—
and they help you reach it faster, too.

One great use of words is to hide our thoughts.

Praise, like gold and diamonds, owes its value to its scarcity.

Heaven is blessed with perfect rest, but the blessing of earth is toil.

True happiness depends upon close alliance with God.

To see God in everything makes life
the greatest adventure there is.

A thankful heart is not only the greatest virtue,
but the parent of all the other virtues.

A sad saint is a sorry saint.

Happiness is the best teacher of good manners;
only the unhappy are churlish.

There is always something wrong with a man, as there is
with a motor, when he knocks continually.

A smile is cheer to you and me
The cost is nothing—it's given free
It comforts the weary—gladdens the sad
Consoles those in trouble—good or bad
To rich and poor—beggar or thief
It's free to all of any belief
A natural gesture of young and old
Cheers on the faint—disarms the bold
Unlike most blessings for which we pray
It's one thing we keep when we give it away.

We must be willing to pay a price for freedom, for no price that
is ever asked for is half the cost of doing without it.

O, I am grown so free from care since my heart broke!

Life and Death are parts of the same great adventure. Do not fear to die and do not shrink from the joy of life.

Sit ye, rock and think.

You may call that your own which no man can take from you.

If we learn how to give ourselves, to forgive others, and to live with thanksgiving, we need not seek happiness—it will seek us.

Gratitude is the memory of the heart.

Sympathy is never wasted except when you give it to yourself.

The man who deals in sunshine is the man
who wins the crowds.
He does a lot more business than the man
who peddles clouds.

Liberty is always dangerous, but it is the safest thing we have.

Winter on her head—Eternal spring in her heart.

Our joys are our wings;
Our sorrows are our spurs.

There is nothing more beautiful than a rainbow,
but it takes both rain and sunshine to make a rainbow. If life
is to be rounded and many-colored like the rainbow, both joy
and sorrow must come to it. Those who have never known anything
but prosperity and pleasure become hard and shallow,
but those whose prosperity has been mixed with adversity
become kind and gracious.

Almost all men improve on acquaintance.

Happiness consists not in possessing much, but in being content with
what we now possess. He who wants little always has enough.

The smile on your face is the light in the window
that tells people that you are at home.

If you don't make a living, live on what you make.

Some men have their first dollar. The man who is really rich
is one who still has his first friend.

Once upon a time I planned to be
An artist of celebrity.
A song I thought to write one day,
And all the world would homage pay.
I longed to write a noted book,
But what I did was—learn to cook.

For life with simple tasks is filled,
And I have done, not what I willed,
Yet when I see boys' hungry eyes
I'm glad I make good apple pies!

The way to be happy is to make others happy.
Helping others is the secret of all success—
in business, in the arts and in the home.

We do not know how cheap the seeds of happiness are
or we should scatter them more often.

To speak kindly does not hurt the tongue.

The nearer she approached the end, the plainer she seemed to hear
round her the immortal symphonies of the world to come.

Dwell on the duty of happiness as well as the happiness of duty.

Happiness is the only thing we can give without having.

The secret of contentment is knowing how to enjoy what you have
and be able to lose all desire for things beyond your reach.

Do not speak of your happiness to one less fortunate
than yourself.

You can't keep trouble from coming, but you needn't give it
a chair to sit on.

Many of us spend half our time wishing for things we could have
if we didn't spend half our time wishing.

All the flowers of all the tomorrows
are in the seeds of today.

I should like to spend the whole of my life traveling, if I could
anywhere borrow another life to live at home.

It is when the holiday is over that we begin to enjoy it.

The light that shines the farthest
shines the brightest nearest home.

The happiness of your life depends upon
the quality of your thoughts.

The glory of life is to love, not to be loved; to give, not to get; to
serve, not to be served.

Pleasures are like poppies spread;
You seize the flower, the bloom is shed.

One of the biggest thrills in life
comes from doing a job well.

Each new day is an opportunity to start all over again . . .
to cleanse our minds and hearts anew and to clarify our vision.
And let us not clutter up today with the leavings
of other days.

PEACE

Take with you words, strong words of courage:
Words that have wings! . . .
Take with you holy words, words that know God:
Words that are sacred as healing waters.
Pure as light, and beautiful as morning,
Take with you tall words, words that reach up,
And growing words, with deep life within them.
Take with you holy words, words that know God.

In His will is our peace.

If there is righteousness in the heart,
there will be beauty in the character,
If there is beauty in the character,
there will be harmony in the home.
If there is harmony in the home,
there will be order in the nation.
If there is order in the nation,
there will be peace in the world.

Man's capacity for justice makes democracy possible; but man's inclination to injustice makes democracy necessary.

Fear God and all other fears will disappear.

In much of my talking, thinking is half-murdered.

If you clutter up your mind with little things, will there by any room left for the big things?

We can never herd the world into the paths of righteousness with the dogs of war.

If humanity could be taught self-control and selfishness-control, there would be no need for atom control.

You are none the holier for being praised, and none the worse for being blamed.

You can't get anywhere today if you are still mired down in yesterday.

The load of tomorrow added to that of yesterday, carried today, makes the strongest falter.

Worry is interest paid on trouble before it is due.

Reality may be a rough road, but escape is a precipice.

Nothing in life is to be feared. It is only to be understood.

He that goes a borrowing goes a sorrowing.

That man is the richest whose pleasures are the cheapest.

The Bible is the book of all others to be read at all ages and in all conditions of human life.

Work is the best narcotic.

Habit is man's best friend or his worst enemy.

Quiet minds cannot be perplexed or frightened but go on in fortune or in misfortune at their own private pace like the ticking of a clock during a thunderstorm.

Our restlessness is largely due to the fact that we are as yet wanderers between two worlds.

Who is wise? He that learns from everyone.
Who is powerful? He that governs his passions.
Who is rich? He that is content.
Who is that? Nobody.

The fellow who worries about what people think of him wouldn't worry so much if he only knew how seldom they do.

Absence of occupation is not rest;
A mind quite vacant is a mind distressed.

He only is advancing in life whose heart is getting softer, his blood warmer, his brain quicker, and his spirit entering into living peace.

No wise man ever wished to be younger.

A clean conscience is a soft pillow.

All the sleepless nights, burdened days, joyless, restless, peace-destroying, health-destroying, happiness-destroying, love-destroying hours men and women have ever in all earth's centuries given to Worry never wrought one good thing!

He who is taught to live upon little owes more to his father's wisdom than he who has a great deal left him does to his father's care.

When you can no longer dwell in the solitude of your heart, you live in your lips and sound is a diversion and a pastime.

Worry never climbed a hill
Worry never paid a bill

Worry never dried a tear
Worry never calmed a fear
Worry never darned a heel
Worry never cooked a meal
Worry never lead a horse to water
Worry never done a thing you'd think it oughta.

There is no conflict between the old and the new; the conflict is
between the false and the true.

It's right to be contented with what you have but never
with what you are.

There is no place to hide a sin,
Without the conscience looking in!

Peace is not the absence of conflict, but the ability
to cope with it.

The rest of our days depends upon the rest of our nights.

Anger is a wind that blows out the lamp of the mind.

Though we travel the world over to find the beautiful, we must
carry it with us or we find it not.

Rest is not quitting the busy career:
Rest is the fitting of self to its sphere.
'Tis loving and serving the highest and best!
'Tis onward unswerving, and that is true rest.

Are you disillusioned with your disillusionments?

Life is a voyage in which we choose neither vessel nor weather,
but much can be done in the management of the sails and
the guidance of the helm.

A good memory is fine—but the ability to forget is
the true test of greatness.

The light that shows us our sin is the light that heals us.

God grant me the serenity to accept the things I cannot change;
the courage to change the things I can; and the wisdom
to know the difference.

To will what God wills brings peace.

Climb the mountains and get their glad tidings. Nature's peace will
flow to you as the sunshine flows into the trees. The winds blow their
own freshness into you, and the storms their energy, while cares drop
away from you like the leaves of autumn.

Not even the perpetually hungry live by bread alone.

Solitude is the ante-chamber of God; only one step more and you
will be in His immediate presence.

Any housewife, no matter how large her family, can always get some
time to be alone by doing the dishes.

Great people are not affected by each puff of wind
that blows ill. Like great ships, they sail serenely on, in a calm sea
or a great tempest.

If you have known how to compose your life,
you have accomplished a great deal more than a man who knows
how to compose a book. Have you been able to take your stride?
You have done more than the man who has taken
cities and empires.

Meditation or medication?

Pray or be a prey—a prey to fears, to futilities,
to ineffectiveness.

You talk when you cease to be at peace
with your thoughts.

A minute of thought is worth more than an hour of talk.

The itching sensation that some people mistake for ambition
is merely inflammation of the wishbone.

To be content with little is difficult,
to be content with much, impossible.

LONG SUFFERING

Much wisdom remains to be learned, and if it is only to be learned through adversity, we must endeavor to endure adversity with what fortitude we can command. But if we can acquire some wisdom soon enough, adversity may not be necessary and the future of man may be happier than any part of his past.

Education is a companion that no misfortune can decrease, no crime destroy, no enemy alienate, no despotism enslave; at home a friend, abroad an introduction, in solitude a solace, in society an ornament. It chastens vice, guides virtue, and gives grace and government to genius. Education may cost financial sacrifice and mental pain, but in both money and life values it will repay every cost one hundred fold.

There is a field for critics, no doubt, but we don't remember seeing statues of any of them in the Hall of Fame.

Why must we have memory enough to recall to the tiniest detail what has happened to us, and not enough to remember how many times we have told it to the same person.

The bird with the broken pinion never soared so high again,
but its song is sweeter!

Whoever has resigned himself to fate, will find that fate
accepts his resignation.

One of the hardest things to teach our children about money matters
is that it does.

If you have learned to walk
A little more sure-footedly than I,
Be patient with my stumbling then
And know that only as I do my best and try
May I attain the goal
for which we both are striving.

If through experience, your soul
Has gained heights which I
As yet in dim-lit vision see,
Hold out your hand and point the way,
Lest from its straightness I should stray,
And walk a mile with me.

Men and automobiles are much alike. Some are right at home on
an uphill pull; others run smoothly only going down-grade, and
when you hear one knocking all the time, it's a sure sign
there is something wrong under the hood.

Charity is injurious unless it helps the recipient to become independent of it.

What we do not understand we do not possess.

Will Power—Won't Power—Supreme Power!

If you never stick your neck out, you'll never get your head above the crowd.

Patience—in time the grass becomes milk.

There is no sense in advertising your troubles. There's no market for them.

Genius is only patience.

He who accepts evil without protesting against it is really cooperating with it.

A man could retire nicely in his old age if he could dispose of his experience for what it cost him.

It is not the ship in the water but the water in the ship that sinks it.

It is not miserable to be blind; it is miserable to be incapable of enduring blindness.

You cannot help men permanently by doing for them what they could and should do for themselves.

Fortune does not change men. It only unmasks them.

Use disappointment as material for patience.

Telling your troubles always helps. The world's dumb indifference makes you mad enough to keep on fighting.

Women are here to stay . . . let's make the best of them.

Those who have suffered much are like those who know many languages; they have learned to understand all and to be understood by all.

The worse thing that happens to a man may be the best thing that ever happened to him if he doesn't let it get the best of him.

There is no failure save in giving up.

Sometimes the best gain is to lose.

A man can fail many times, but he isn't a failure until he begins to blame somebody else.

Forget mistakes. Organize victory out of mistakes.

All problems become smaller if you don't dodge them but confront them. Touch a thistle timidly and it will prick you; grasp it boldly and its spines crumble.

He who strikes the first blow confesses he has run out of ideas.

A man's best fortune or his worst is his wife.

When you're through changing, you're through.

The diamond cannot be polished without friction, nor man perfected without trials.

Trying times are times for trying.

Education should be as gradual as the moonrise, perceptible not in progress but in result.

Why value the present hour less than some future hour?

The secret of patience is doing something else in the meanwhile.

If you don't scale the mountain, you can't see the view.

Trouble is only opportunity in work clothes.

Only one person in the whole wide world can defeat you.
That is yourself!

Like a hick'ry cog
In the old mill wheel,
He did his part
As his turn came 'round.

I had no shoes and complained until I met a man who had no feet.

Before you flare up at anyone's faults, take time to count to ten—
ten of your own.

We are never more discontented with others than when we are
discontented with ourselves.

The door to the room of success swings on the hinges of opposition.

It isn't the load that weights us down—it's the way we carry it.

The greatest calamity is not to have failed:
but to have failed to try.

The only time you mustn't fail is the last time you try.

A diamond is a piece of coal that stuck to the job.

God never makes us conscious of our weakness except to give us
of his strength.

There is nothing wrong with the younger generation
that twenty years won't cure.

Stars may be seen from the bottom of a deep well, when they cannot
be seen from the top of the mountain. So are many things learned in
adversity, which the prosperous man dreams not of.

Perhaps the most valuable result of all education is the ability
to make ourselves do the thing we have to do when it ought to be
done, whether we like it or not.

The hardest thing of all in life—
The conquest not of time and space,
But of ourselves, of our stupidity and inertia,
Of our greediness and touchiness,
Of our fear and intolerant dogmatism.

The difference between stumbling blocks and stepping stones
is the ways a man uses them.

Every time you give another a "piece of your mind" you add
to your own vacuum.

We cannot do everything at once; but we can do something at once.

No horse gets anywhere till he is harnessed. No steam ever drives
anything until it is confined. No Niagara is ever turned into light and
power until it is tunneled. No life ever grows great until it is focused,
dedicated, disciplined.

When the archer misses the center of the target he seeks for
the cause within himself.

The world is made better by every man improving his own conduct;
and no reform is accomplished wholesale.

The most difficult year of marriage is the one you're in.

Life is 10% what you make it and 90% how you take it.

Be not angry that you cannot make others as you wish them to be
since you cannot make yourself as you wish to be.

Itching for what you want doesn't do much good;
you've got to scratch for it.

He who has learned to disagree without being disagreeable
has discovered the most valuable secret of a diplomat.

Your ulcers are not due to what you are eatin'
but to what's eatin' you.

Better to let 'em wonder why you didn't talk than why you did.

We would rather be ruined by praise than saved by criticism.

If at first you don't succeed, you are running about average.

Do not be disturbed at being misunderstood. Be disturbed
at not understanding.

Our country, right or wrong!
When right, to be kept right;
When wrong, to be put right.

You've reached middle age when all you exercise is caution.

It takes the whole of life to learn how to live.

Housework is something you do that nobody notices
unless you don't do it.

It isn't the mountain ahead that wears you out—it's the grain of sand
in your shoe.

The highest reward that God gives us for good work is
the ability to do better.

Everything comes to him who waits, if he works while he waits.

Injustice is relatively easy to bear; what stings is justice.

Do not go to pieces if you burn the toast. Some day your house may
burn down and you can take that calmly too.

Marrying is not marriage.

No one can work me injury but myself.

To be thrown upon one's resources is to be cast into the
very lap of fortune.

The trouble with some people is that they won't admit their faults. I'd
admit mine—if I had any.

The Lord sometimes takes us into troubled waters NOT to drown us,
but to cleanse us.

Try to fix the mistake—never the blame.

To sin by silence when they should protest, makes cowards of men.

The world is not interested in the storms you encountered—
but did you bring in the ship?

I'd better not be wasting Time,
For Time is wasting me!

Just about the time you think you can make both ends meet,
somebody moves the ends.

Education isn't play and it can't be made to look like play. It is hard,
hard work, but it can be made interesting work.

Talent may develop in solitude, but character is developed in society.

The more difficult the obstacle, the stronger one becomes
after hurdling it.

Fault finders never improve the world: they only make it seem worse
than it really is.

Taxes could be much worse—suppose we had to pay
on what we think we're worth.

A failure is a man who has blundered but is not able to
cash in the experience.

Failure is endeavor, and endeavor persisted in is never failure.

Learn from the mistakes of others—you can't live long enough
to make them all yourself.

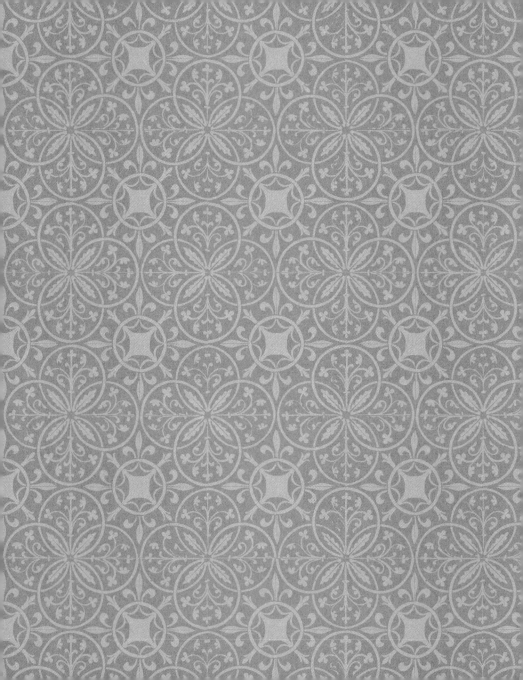

GENTLENESS

This book can be like a well-chosen and well-tended
fruit tree. Its fruits are not of one season only.
With the due and natural intervals, you may recur to it
year after year, and it will supply the same nourishment
and the same gratification, if only you return to it
with the same healthy appetite.

So many gods, so many creeds,
So many paths that wind and wind;
When just the art of being kind
Is all the sad world needs.

The kindly word that falls today may bear its fruit tomorrow.

A good manner springs from a good heart, and fine manners
are the outcome of unselfish kindness.

One cannot find any rule of conduct to excel
"simplicity" and "sincerity."

Every noble life leaves the fiber of it interwoven
in the woof of the world.

He who influences the thought of his time influences the thought
of all the times that follow.

The blossom cannot tell what becomes of its odor and no man
can tell what becomes of his influence and example that roll away
from him and go beyond his view.

Only the best behavior is good enough for daily use in the home.

Nothing is so strong as gentleness, nothing so gentle
as real strength.

A candle-glow can pierce the darkest night.

A gentleman is a gentle man.

Speech may sometimes do harm; but so may silence and a worse harm
at that. No insult ever caused so deep a wound as a tenderness
expected and withheld; and no spoken indiscretion was ever so
bitterly regretted as the word that one did not speak.

Be what you wish others to become.

Be to his virtues very kind.
Be to his faults very blind.

One learns manners from those who have none.

An admission of error is a sign of strength,
rather than a confession of weakness.

If you confer a benefit, never remember it;
If you receive one, never forget it.

Be kind, for everyone you meet is fighting a hard battle.

GOODNESS

We are all manufacturers, making goods, making trouble
or making excuses.

A little thing is a little thing, but faithfulness in little things
is a great thing.

Character is property—it is the noblest of possessions.

The highest reward for a man's toil is not what he gets for it,
but rather what he becomes by it.

It is not so much what a man is descended from that matters
as what he will descend to.

Truth is the foundation of all knowledge and
the cement of all societies.

You can preach a better sermon with your life than with your lips.

Praise not only pretends that we are better than we are; it may help
to make us better than we are.

Good depends not on things, but on the use we make of things.

Life is too short to be little.

To the man in us, time is a quantity;
To the God in us, it is a quality.

To do the right thing for the wrong reason is the greatest treason.

Who worships Christ in bread and wine,
And kneels before the High and Pure,
Meets Him again in street and mine
And in the faces of the poor.

You are writing a gospel,
A chapter each day,
by deeds that you do,
By words that you say.
Men read what you write,
Whether faithless or true,
Say, what is the gospel according to you?

The only way to settle a disagreement is on the basis
of what's right—not who's right.

What I must do, and not what people think, is all that concerns me.

Silver and gold are not the only coin; virtue also passes
all over the world.

Your luck is how you treat people.

The measure of man's real character is what he would do if he knew
he would never be found out.

See each person you meet as one who knows your Lord
or is seeking your Lord.

We search the world for truth, we cull
The good, the true, the beautiful,
From graven stone and written scroll,
And all old flower-fields of the soul;
And, weary seekers of the best,
We come back laden from our quest,
To find that all the sages said
Is in the Book our mothers read.

We have committed the golden Rule to memory; let us now
commit it to life.

The greatest distance we have yet to cover still lies within us.

A man is rich according to what he is, not according to what he has.

A good example is the best sermon.

The world is slowly learning that because two men think differently
neither need be wicked.

The Golden Rule—not the rule of gold.

Children need models more than they need critics.

Life lived just to satisfy yourself never satisfies anybody.

There is no better exercise for strengthening the heart than
reaching down and lifting people up.

What lies behind us and what lies before us are tiny matters
compared to what lies within us.

Character is a victory, not a gift.

There is no right way to do the wrong thing.

Whatever creed be taught or land be trod,
Man's conscience is the oracle of God.

What I am to be I am now becoming.

The hardest job that people have to do is to move religion from their throats to their muscles.

A living religion is a way of living.

A man's reputation is only what men think him to be; his character is what God knows him to be.

Goodness is the only investment that never fails.

Though another may have more money, beauty, brains than you; yet when it comes to the rarer spiritual values such as charity, self-sacrifice, honor, nobility of heart, you have an equal chance with everyone to be the most beloved and honored of all people.

The real purpose of our existence is not to make a living, but to make a life—a worthy, well-rounded, useful life.

Do all the good you can
By all the means you can
In all the ways you can
In all the places you can
At all the times you can
To all the people you can
As long as ever you can.

Christian character is not an inheritance; each individual
must build it for himself.

What you are in the sight of God, that you truly are.

To clear difficulties out of the way, there is no axe
like a good principle.

Are you easing the load of overtaxed lifters who toil down the road?
Or, are you a leaner who lets others share your portion of labor,
worry and care?

Good nature will always supply the absence of beauty; but beauty
cannot supply the absence of good nature.

Be the true man you seek.

Nothing that is morally wrong can ever be politically correct.

My part is to improve the present moment.

Do right and leave the results with God.

The difference between a prejudice and a conviction is that you can
explain a conviction without getting mad.

To become Christlike is the only thing in the whole world worth caring for; the thing before which every ambition of man is folly, and all lower achievement vain.

It will not be easy to brainwash the heartwashed.

Democracy means not "I am equal to you" but "you are equal to me."

It is often surprising to find what heights may be attained merely by remaining on the level.

It is hard for the good to suspect evil as it is for the bad to suspect good.

The Devil has many tools, but a lie is the handle that fits them all.

If you blame others for your failures, do you credit others with your successes?

There isn't any map on the road to success; you have to find your own way.

He who is not liberal with what he has deceives himself when he thinks he would be liberal if he had more.

Are you trying to make something for yourself
or something of yourself?

A lie has no legs. It requires other lies to support it. Tell one lie and
you are forced to tell others to back it up.

A good man does not hesitate to own he has been in the wrong. He
takes comfort in knowing he is wiser today than he was yesterday.

Stretching the truth won't make it last any longer.

The only wise speed at which to live is . . . Godspeed.

I have resolved never to do anything that I should be afraid to do if it
were the last hour of my life.

FAITH

Faith is a gift of God. It is not a material that can be seen,
heard, smelled, tasted, or touched; but is as real as anything
that can be perceived with these senses. One can be aware of Faith as
easily as one can be aware of earth. Faith is as certain as is the
existence of water. Faith is as sure as the taste of an apple,
the fragrance of a rose, the sound of thunder, the sight of the sun,
the feel of a loving touch. Hope is a wish, a longing for something
not now possessed, but with the expectation of getting it.
Faith adds surety to the expectation of hope.

Today is the tomorrow you worried about yesterday.

I am to be so busy today that I must spend more time than usual
in prayer.

Inexperience is what makes a young man do what an older man
says is impossible.

When you get to the end of your rope, tie a knot in it
and hang on.

You are not a reservoir with a limited amount of resources; you are a channel attached to unlimited divine resources.

God is playing chess with man. He meets his every move.

The sectarian thinks that he has the sea ladled into his private pond.

Who draws nigh to God through doubtings dim . . . God will advance a mile in blazing light to him.

I am only one, but I am one. I cannot do everything, but I can do something; and what I should do and can do, by the Grace of God I will do.

No vision and you perish
No ideal and you are lost,
Your heart must ever cherish
Some faith at any cost.

Anyone can carry his burden, however heavy, until nightfall; anyone can do his work, however hard, for one day.

Prayer is not overcoming God's reluctance; it is laying hold on His willingness.

Prayer is not an attitude attained but an attitude maintained.

The secret of prayer is secret prayer.

The man who trusts men will make fewer mistakes
than he who distrusts them.

God's requirements are met by God's enablings.

A skeptic is one who won't take know for an answer.

I have faith in Him, not in my faith.

No man is responsible for the rightness of his faith; but only
for the uprightness of it.

Dare to be wise: begin! He who postpones the hour of living rightly
is like the rustic who waits for the river to run out
before he crosses.

The night is not forever.

Do not worry about whether or not the sun will rise;
be prepared to enjoy it.

The best and most beautiful things in the world cannot be seen nor
touched but are felt in the heart.

The Christian on his knees sees more than the philosopher on tiptoe.

Nothing costs so much as what is bought by prayers.

It is better to suffer wrong than to do it, and happier to sometimes be cheated than not to trust.

God never closes one door without opening another.

Faith is the grave of care.

Prayer is not a substitute for work. It is a desperate effort to work further and to be effective beyond the range of one's power.

We are always complaining our days are few, and acting as though there would be no end of them.

The past cannot be changed; the future is still in your power.

O, Lord, help me to understand that you ain't gwine to let nuthin' come my way that you and me together can't handle.

What you can do, or dream you can, begin it.
Courage has genius, power and magic in it;
Only engage, and then the mind grows heated.
Begin it and the work will be completed.

Some people can see at a glance what others cannot see
with searchlights and telescopes.

The best evidence of the Bible's being the Word of God is to be found
between its covers.

Life is easier than you think. All you have to do
is accept the impossible, do without the indispensable,
and bear the intolerable.

Prayer without work is beggary;
Work without prayer is slavery.

What are you saving in your memory bin as food for the restless soul
when the winter of life comes?

I'll take the Bible as my guide until something better comes along.

For a web begun, God sends thread.

Life is eternal, Love is immortal and Death is only an horizon and an
horizon is only the limit of our sight.

Instead of waiting upon the Lord, some people want the Lord
to wait upon them.

This body is my house—it is not I.
Triumphant in this faith I live and die.

Satan trembles when he sees the weakest saint
upon his knees.

To pray "Thy will be done" should be no attitude of passive
submission but a call to the whole nature to strive to do
the utmost for the cause of God.

With God, go even over the sea;
without Him, not over the threshold.

With God, nothing shall be impossible.

It is not the lazy who are most inclined to prayer;
those pray most who care most, and who, having worked hard,
find it intolerable to be defeated.

Don't tell me that worry doesn't do any good. I know better.
The things I worry about don't happen.

If a man has any religion, he must give it up or give it away.

Do the very best you can . . . and leave the outcome to God.

I know not what the future hath of marvel or surprise,
assured alone that life and death His mercy underlies.

The trivial round, our common task,
Would furnish all we ought to ask;
Room to deny ourselves; a road
To bring us daily nearer God.

Real prayer always does one of two things: It either frees us
from the trouble we fear or else it gives us the strength and courage
to meet the trouble when it comes.

One on God's side is a majority.

Are your troubles causing you to lose your religion
or use your religion?

Wit's end need not be the end, but the beginning. The end of man's
contriving often is the beginning of God's arriving.

Life left to God
Will bring a greater yield
Of golden harvest and of ripened field
Than all the weary plannings of thy soul
Can force to be, or strength of will control;
Oh, trust a Power that must bring good from all,
And leave thy life to God!

If a psychologist assures me that I believe in God because
of the way my nurse used to treat me, I must reply that he only
holds that belief concerning my belief because of
the way in which his nurse used to treat him.

Why is it opportunities always look bigger going than coming?

All I see teaches me to trust the Creator for all I do not see.

If seeds in the black earth can turn into such beautiful roses,
what might not the heart of man become in its long journey
toward the stars?

Of all the troubles great and small are those that
never happened at all.

The Bible is a guidebook; the way to master it is to let it master us.

Freedom rests, and always will, on individual responsibility,
individual integrity, individual effort, individual courage,
and individual religious faith.

Man's extremity is God's opportunity.

If there is no way out, there is a way up.

This is what I found about religion: It gives you courage to make the decisions you must make in a crisis, and then the confidence to leave the result to a higher power. Only by trust in God can a man carrying responsibility find repose.

A wish is a desire without any attempt to attain its end.

It is difficult to pray because it is difficult to know what we ought to desire.

It is only the fear of God that can deliver us from the fear of men.

Morale is when your hands and feet keep on working when your head says it can't be done.

Death is not extinguishing the light; it is putting out the lamp because dawn has come.

Out of the seed the flower ;
Out of the flower the seed;
Out of the need the power;
Out of the power the deed.

Only he who can see the invisible can do the impossible.

Do you pray, and then believing,
Grab your boots and parasol;
Scrub the barrel and get ready
For the rain you asked to fall?

Don't be afraid to be afraid.

He says not, "at the end of the way you find ME." he says,
"I AM the way: I AM the road under your feet, the road
that begins just as low as you happen to be."

Be patient enough to live one day at a time as Jesus taught us,
letting yesterday go and leaving tomorrow until it arrives.

Instead of fearing death, we should look it in the face and
recognize it for what it is—a friend that has come to release us
from the bondage of the flesh.

Lord, I shall be very busy this day. I may forget Thee . . . But
do not Thou forget me.

We plant a tree this day and leave the blossoming to God.

Fear brings more pain than does the pain it fears.

All the fitness He requireth is to feel your need of Him.

Does your faith move mountains, or do mountains move your faith?

Prayer should be the key of the day and the lock of the night.

Do you have invisible means of support?

Our doubts are traitors and make us lose the good oft we might win,
by fearing to attempt.

If you must doubt, doubt your doubts—never your beliefs.

A man is not old until regrets take the place of dreams.

Cease to inquire what the future has in store, but take as a gift
whatever the day brings forth.

Nothing is all wrong. Even a clock that has stopped running
is right twice a day.

No world left to conquer? The frontiers of the mind are just beginning
to be discovered, and the spiritual world surrounding us yet remains
a complete mystery.

First do more than you are paid for before expecting to be paid for
more than you do.

Prayer digs the channels from the reservoir of God's boundless resources to the tiny pools of our lives.

There is no greater obstacle in the way of success in life than trusting for something to turn up, instead of going to work and turning up something.

I never knew a night so black
Light failed to follow on its track.
I never knew a storm so gray,
It failed to have its clearing day.
I never knew such bleak despair,
That there was not a rift, somewhere.
I never knew an hour so drear,
Love could not fill it full of cheer.

Some folks just don't seem to realize when they're moaning about not getting prayers answered, that NO is the answer.

Life is hard, by the yard;
But by the inch, life's a cinch!

The task of spiritual science: Discover the little acorns out of which big oaks grow and provide room for the growth of such mighty trees.

We can easily forgive a child who is afraid of the dark. The real tragedy of life is when men are afraid of the Light.

Without the way, there is no going;
Without the truth, there is no knowing;
Without the life, there is no living.

The world is moved not only by the mighty shoves of the heroes, but
also by the aggregate of the tiny pushes of each honest worker.

He didn't know it couldn't be done but went ahead and did it.

A traveler crossed a frozen stream
In trembling fear one day;
Later a teamster drove across,
And whistled all the way.

Great faith and little faith alike
Were granted safe convoy;
One had the pangs of needless fear,
The other all the joy.

It is not the greatness of my faith that moves mountains, but my faith
in the greatness of God.

You can't control the length of your life—but you can control its
width and depth. You can't control the contour of your face—but you
can control its expression. You can't control the atmosphere of your
mind. Why worry about things you can't control when you can keep
yourself busy controlling the things that depend on you.

People believe what they want to believe despite all the evidence to the contrary.

As is your "Amen" so is your prayer.

Prayer changes things. Prayer changes you!

He who loses money loses much; he who loses a friend loses more, but he who loses faith loses all.

The only ideas that will work for you are the ones you put to work.

God without man is still God.
Man without God is nothing.

When we see the lilies spinning in distress,
Taking thought to manufacture loveliness—
When we see the birds all building barns for store,
'Twill be time for us to worry, not before.

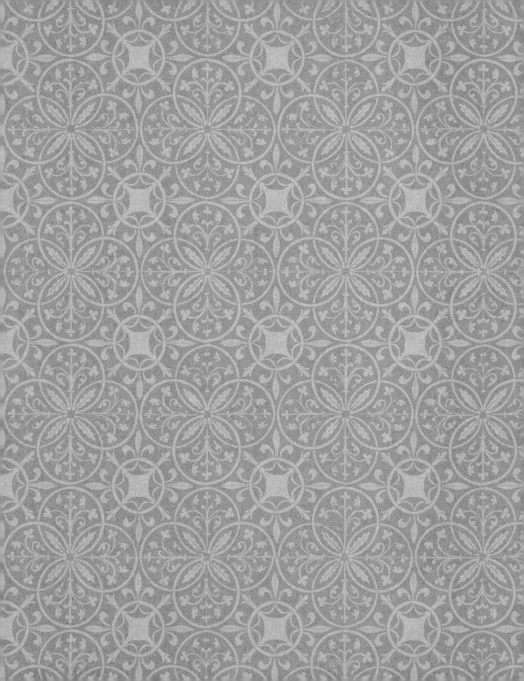

MEEKNESS

Have courage to be ignorant of a great number of things, in order
to avoid the calamity of being ignorant of everything.

The only conquests that are permanent, and leave no regrets,
are conquests over ourselves.

Resiliency is an important factor in living. The winds of life
may bend us, but if we have resilience of spirit, they cannot
break us. To courageously straighten again after our heads
have been bowed by defeat, disappointment, and suffering
is the supreme test of character.

To know how to grow old is the master work of wisdom, and one of
the most difficult chapters in the great art of living.

The best medicine for you to take is yourself—with a grain of salt.

It is with narrow-souled people as with narrow-necked bottles—
the less they have in them the more noise they make
in pouring it out.

There is only one person with whom you can profitably compare yourself, and this person is your yesterday self; You.

The greatest undeveloped territory in the world lies under your hat.

Discussion is an exchange of knowledge: argument is an exchange of ignorance.

Wisdom is to know what is best worth knowing and to do what is best worth doing.

If we resist our passions, it is more through their weakness than our strength.

Conscience is the still small voice that makes you feel still smaller.

The doorstep to the temple of wisdom is a knowledge of our own ignorance.

To be conscious that you are ignorant is a great step toward knowledge.

Never forget that you are a part of the people who can be fooled some of the time.

Don't drive as if you own the road; drive as if you own the car.

Teach thy tongue to say, "I do not know."

A juvenile delinquent is a boy who does what you did
when young, but gets caught.

There is nothing permanent but change.

The best way to succeed in life is to act on the advice
you give to others.

A peck of common sense is worth a bushel of learning.

The bigger a man's head gets, the easier it is to fill his shoes.

Past experience should be a guide post, not a hitching post.

The end of wisdom is to dream high enough not to lose the dream
in the seeking of it.

There's nothing wrong with being a self-made man if
you don't consider the job finished too soon.

The aim of education is to enable a man to continue his learning.

Life is like a ladder: Every step we take is either up or down.

What a fool does in the end, the wise man does in the beginning.

A college education seldom hurts a man if he's willing to learn
a little something after he graduates.

Swallowing your pride occasionally will never give you indigestion.

A philosopher is someone who always knows what to do
until it happens to him.

I am not conceited, though I do have every reason to be.

The steam that blows the whistle can't be used to turn the wheels.

Manhood, not scholarship, is the first aim of education.

When success turns a person's head, he is facing failure.

Men are wise in proportion not to their experience
but to their capacity for experience.

No experienced man ever stigmatized a change of opinion
as inconsistency.

Education does not mean teaching people to know what they do not know; it means teaching them to behave as they do not behave.

Quite often when a man thinks his mind is getting broader it is only his conscience stretching.

Opinions that are well rooted should grow and change like a healthy tree.

Lord, give me this day my daily opinion, and forgive the one I had yesterday.

I thoroughly believe in a university education for both men and women, but I believe a knowledge of the Bible without a college course is more valuable than a college course without a knowledge of the Bible.

Many might have attained wisdom had they not thought that they had already attained it.

The taller a bamboo grows, the lower it bends.

Seems as if some people grow with responsibility—others just swell.

Every man I meet is in some way my superior; and in that I can learn from him.

When you know a thing, to hold that you know it, and when you do not know it, to admit that you do not—this is true knowledge.

The more you know, the more you know you don't know.

To admit I have been in the wrong is but saying that I am wiser today than I was yesterday.

It makes a man sort of humble to have been a kid when everything was the kid's fault and a parent at a time when everything is the parent's fault.

The greatest friend of truth is time,
And her constant companion is humility.

To err may be human, but to admit it isn't.

The purpose of education is to provide everyone with the opportunity to learn how best he may serve the world.

Nothing gives a man more leisure time than being punctual.

Wisdom consists in knowing what to do with what you know.

A learned man has always wealth within himself.

Investment in knowledge pays the best interest.

The man who trims himself to suit everybody will soon
whittle himself away.

The righteous cannot rise beyond the highest which is in me so the
wicked and the weak cannot fall lower than the lowest in me.

Everyone is ignorant—only on different subjects.

Humility is a strange thing. The minute you think you've got it,
you've lost it.

When young, consider that one day you will be old and when old,
remember you were once young.

A man wrapped up in himself makes a very small bundle.

They that know God will be humble; they that know themselves
cannot be proud.

If you want to put the world right, start with yourself.

It is indeed a desirable thing to be well descended, but the glory
belongs to our ancestors.

A college graduate is a person who had a chance to get an education.

Tolerance comes with age. I see no fault committed that I myself could not have committed at some time or other.

The greatest of faults is to be conscious of none.

Nonchalance is the ability to look like an owl when you have acted like a jackass.

When a man gets too old to set a bad example, he starts giving good advice.

An open mind leaves a chance for someone to drop a worthwhile thought in it.

A diplomat is one who can tell a man he's open minded when he means he has a hole in his head.

We see things not as they are, but as we are.

The best thing for gray hair is a sensible head.

Time cannot be expanded, accumulated, mortgaged, hastened, or retarded.

Women will remain the weaker sex just as long as they're smarter.

It is my privilege to profit by the experience of others, but I must live my own life, face the trials, and gain the victory alone.

Most people's hindsight is 20/20.

Every other kind of iniquity prompts the doing of evil deeds, but pride lurks even in good deeds to their undoing.

Are you sure that you are right?
How fine and strong!
But were you ever just as sure—
And wrong?

Flattery is something nice someone tells you about yourself that you wish were true.

It is better to understand a little than to misunderstand a lot.

TEMPERANCE

Where there is an open mind, there will always be a frontier.

The longer you keep your temper the more it will improve.

It's smart to pick your friends—but not to pieces.

Fine eloquence consists in saying all that should be,
not all that could be said.

Wise men are not always silent, but know when to be.

We always have time enough if we but use it aright.

Frugality is good if liberality be joined by it.

It's not that I spend more than I earn, it's just that
I spend it quicker than I earn it.

There is only a slight difference between keeping your chin up and sticking your neck out, but it's worth knowing.

The hand that lifts "the cup that cheers" should not be used to shift the gears.

The driver is safer when the roads are dry; the roads are safer when the driver is dry.

Be sure your brain is in gear before engaging your mouth.

Blessed is he who, having nothing to say, refrains from giving wordy evidence of the fact.

If your dollar won't do as much as it once did, consider: are you doing as much as you once did for a dollar?

Laziness travels so slowly that poverty soon overtakes him.

A man's difficulties begin when he is able to do as he likes.

As easy as falling off a diet.

Gossip is the art of saying nothing in a way that leaves nothing unsaid.

Words in haste do friendships waste.

Silence is a talent as greatly to be cherished as that other asset, the gift of speech.

"A soft answer turneth away wrath" is the best system of self-defense.

People who fly into a rage always make a bad landing.

Often the difference between a successful marriage and a mediocre one consists of leaving about three or four things a day unsaid.

We need mental separators that take off the few ounces of cream that are fit to be spoken to others.

Tact is the unsaid part of what you think.

In any controversy the instant we feel anger we have already ceased striving for truth, and have begun striving for ourselves.

Thrift is a wonderful virtue—especially in ancestors.

It is better to keep your mouth shut and be thought a fool than it is to open it and prove it.

The best victory is to conquer self.

Dignity is the capacity to hold back on the tongue
what never should have been in the mind in the first place.

To cease smoking is the easiest thing I ever did. I ought to know
for I've done it a thousand times.

Habit is a cable; we weave a thread of it every day, and at last
we cannot break it.

Choose the best life, for habit will make it pleasant.

The test of good manners is being able to put up pleasantly
with bad ones.

In times of crisis we must avoid both ignorant changes
and ignorant opposition to change.

Even moderation ought not to be practiced to excess.

Out of the mouths of babes come words we shouldn't have said
in the first place.

You can never tell about a woman, and if you can, you shouldn't.

Who gossips to you will gossip of you.

The real problem of your leisure is how to keep other people from using it.

Better to slip with the foot than with the tongue.

The archer who overshoots his mark does no better than he who falls short of it.

Economy is an important virtue and debt can be a danger to be feared.

Besides the noble art of getting things done, there is the noble art of leaving things undone. The wisdom of life consists in the elimination of nonessentials.

Do you act or react?

We always weaken what we exaggerate.

There is nothing wrong with making mistakes, but don't respond to encores.

Your body is for use—not abuse.

If silence be good for wise men, how much better
must it be for fools.

Do you spend more than you make on things you don't need
to impress people you don't like?

No echoes return to mock the silent tongue.

I have often regretted my speech, seldom my silence.

It's all right to hold a conversation, but you should let go
of it now and then.

If your outgo exceeds your income, then your upkeep
will be your downfall.

Man is master of the unspoken word, which, spoken,
is master of him.

Speech is the index of the mind.

Money may not go as far as it used to, but we have
just as much trouble getting it back.

A loose tongue often gets into a tight place.

Too many people quit looking for work when they find a job.

Ideas are funny little things. They won't work unless you do.

Sooner throw a pearl at hazard than an idle or useless word; and do not say a little in many words, but a great deal in a few.

Everything has been thought of before . . . the difficulty is to think of it again.

WINGS OF SILVER

LOVE • JOY • PEACE
LONG SUFFERING
GENTLENESS • GOODNESS
FAITH • MEEKNESS • TEMPERANCE

LOVE

Love suffers long, and is kind;
Love envies not;
Love vaunts not itself, is not puffed up;
Does not behave itself unseemly,
Seeks not her own,
Is not easily provoked,
Thinks no evil,
Rejoices not in iniquity, but rejoices in the truth;
Bears all things,
Believes all things,
Hopes all things,
Endures all things,
Love never fails!

We dare not violate the law of love any more than
we can defy the law of gravitation.

The test of our love to God is the love we have one for another.

The language of love is understood by all.

Love ever gives and forgives.

All loves should be stepping stones to the love of God.

Love is the commandment for fulfilling all commandments—
the rule for fulfilling all rules.

Love works no ill to his neighbor; therefore, love
is the fulfilling of the law.

We love ourselves notwithstanding our faults, and we ought
to love our friends in like manner.

When a friend asks, there is no tomorrow.

If you love, you love others and yourself.
If you hate, you hate others and yourself.

Love never reasons but profusely gives, gives like a thoughtless
prodigal its all, and trembles then lest it has done too little.

Love knows no limit to its endurance, no end to its trust,
no fading of its hope; it can outlast anything. Love still stands
when all else has fallen.

Love that has ends will have an end.

We know that all things work together for good
to them that love God.

How shall I do to love? Believe. How shall I do to believe? Love.

By your love to God, the love to your neighbor is begotten, and by
the love to your neighbor, your love to God is nourished.

The greatest happiness of life is the conviction that we are loved,
loved for ourselves, or rather loved in spite of ourselves.

Love is the root of all virtues.

If there is anything better than to be loved, it is loving.

If we love one another, God dwells in us.

Are we willing to be made willing to forgive?

If our love were but more simple,
We should take Him at His word,
And our lives would be all sunshine
In the sweetness of the Lord.

He that loves his brother abides in the light.

Hate is sand in the machinery of life—love is oil.

Love is love's reward.

Hatred is like an acid. It can do more damage to the vessel in which
it is stored than to the object on which it is poured.

God so loved the world that He gave His only begotten Son,
that whosoever believeth in Him should not perish,
but have everlasting life.

The solutions to all our problems are more of the heart
than of the law.

Love is to the moral nature what the sun is to the earth.

The husband or wife who harvests thorns
should look to his or her gardening. Either responds
to steadfast love like a plant in the sunshine, sprouting
new dimensions to his or her personality
on the side where the sun shines brightest.

Love and you shall be loved.

Love understands, and love waits.

Love, like warmth, should beam forth on every side and bend
to every necessity of our brothers.

He prays best who loves best.

Never undervalue any person—the workman loves not to have
his work despised in his presence. Now God is present everywhere,
and every person is His work.

Not where I breathe, but where I love, I live.

Fall in love with yourself and you have no rivals.

Who shall separate us from the love of Christ? Shall tribulation, or
distress, or persecution, or famine, or nakedness, or peril, or sword?

The quarrels of lovers are like summer storms. Everything is more
beautiful when they have passed.

I hold him great who for love's sake
Can give with earnest, generous will.
But he who takes for love's sweet sake,
I think I hold more generous still.

Husbands, love your wives, even as Christ also loved the Church and
gave Himself for it.

Never marry but for love; but see that you love what is lovely.

The bravest battle that was ever fought;
Shall I tell you where and when?
On the maps of the world you will find it not;
It was fought by the mothers of men.

The remedy for wrongs is to forget them.

Has some resentment
wrought strife and ill-will?
Love and forgiveness
work miracles still.

Be kindly affectioned one to another with brotherly love;
in honor preferring one another.

Be charitable before wealth makes you covetous.

Love your enemies, and do good, and lend, hoping for nothing again;
and your reward shall be great, and you shall be the children of the
Highest: for He is kind unto the unthankful and to the evil.

Love your enemies, for they tell you your faults.

We must love our fellow man because God loves him and will to
redeem him.

Whoever in prayer can say "Our Father" acknowledges and should
feel the brotherhood of the whole race of mankind.

He who despises, despises not men, but God.

You should love your neighbor as yourself, and
you should be good to yourself.

Owe no man anything, but to love one another; for he
that loves another has fulfilled the law.

Science has made the world a neighborhood, but it will take religion
to make it a brotherhood.

Who loves God loves his brother also.

Add to your faith virtue; and to virtue knowledge; and to knowledge
temperance; and to temperance patience; and to patience godliness;
and to godliness brotherly kindness; and to brotherly kindness LOVE!

This is the message that you have heard from the beginning,
that we should love one another.

Being rooted and grounded in love, we are able to comprehend
the breadth, and length, and depth, and height, and
to know the love of Christ, which passes knowledge,
and to be filled with the fullness of God.

Nothing is hardship to love and nothing is hard.

The brightest blaze of intelligence is of less value
than the smallest spark of charity.

Knowledge puffs up, love builds up.

The greatest pleasure of life is love.

Charity gives itself rich; covetousness hoards itself poor.

The injuries we do, and those we suffer, are seldom weighed
in the same balance.

How empty learning,
How vain is art
But as it mends the life
And guides the heart.

There is no instinct like that of the heart.

Set your affection on things above, and not on things on the earth.

God knows us better than we know ourselves,
and He loves us better, too.

Hate is spiritual suicide.

A child's definition of house and home: "When you are outside, it looks like a house but when you are inside, it feels like a home."

Let us love in deed and truth, rather than in word and tongue.

Increase and abound in love, one toward another,
and toward all men.

Only a thought, but the work it wrought,
Can never by tongue or pen be taught,
for it ran through life like a thread of gold
And the life bore fruit a hundred fold.

Only a word! but 'twas spoken in love,
With a whispered prayer to the Lord above—
and the angels in heaven rejoiced once more,
For a new-born soul entered through the door.

The word of alms is singular, as if to teach us that a solitary act of charity scarcely deserves the name.

Where there is room in the heart there is always room in the house.

Service can be given wherever there are people.

If God so loved us, we ought also to love one another.

A true friend is forever a friend.

Love grows stronger for those who walk with us
day by day.

Love one another.

Herein is love, not that we loved God, but that He loved us
and sent His Son to be the propitiation for our sins.

We pardon as long as we love.

Hatred stirs up strifes; but love covers all sins.

God is love, and he that dwells in love dwells in God,
and God in him.

Love sees what no eye sees; love hears what no ear hears.

The heart has reasons that reason does not understand.

By this shall all men know that ye are My disciples,
if ye have love one to the other.

Many waters cannot quench love, neither can the floods drown it.

No disguise can long conceal love where it is, nor feign it
where it is not.

All God's laws are God's loves.

A loving heart is the truest wisdom.

Of him that hopes to be forgiven, it is required that he forgive.

There is no fear in love; but perfect love casts out fear.

Are we giving the kind of love we seek from God?

Teach me, Father, when I pray,
Not to ask for more,
But rather let me give my thanks
For what is at my door.
For food and drink, for gentle rain,
For sunny skies above,
For home and friends, for peace and joy,
But most of all for love.

Is your love patient and kind? Is it able to suffer long, to endure every
strain placed upon it in human relations, and still love? Is your love as

steadfast in pointing to God's love as is the needle of the compass in pointing to the north? Is your love undiscouraged even by repeated ingratitude and recurrent failures on the part of others? Patience and kindness are the fruits of having Christ live in you. Are you nourishing your life upon His life by prayer and worship and studying His word? If so, the fruit of patient and kind love will grow and well be available for the healing of other lives.

We cannot give like God, but surely we may forgive like Him.

To love is to place our happiness in the happiness of another.

Love not the world, neither the things that are in the world. If any man love the world, the love of the Father is not in him.

There are shadow friendships that appear only when the sun shines.

Open rebuke is better than secret love.

JOY

Happiness is good.
The place to be happy is here.
The time to be happy is now.
The way to be happy is to help make others happy.

Good cheer is no hindrance to a good life.

Only the active have the true relish of life.

Sing with gladness,
Banish your sadness.

The gladness of the heart is the life of man, and the joyfulness of man
prolongs his days.

No entertainment is so cheap as reading, nor any pleasure so lasting.

The love of reading enables a man to exchange the wearisome hours
of life, which come to every one, for hours of delight.

Enjoy present pleasures in such a way as not to injure future ones.

Scorn a pleasure that gives another pain.

Happiness is neither within us only, or without us; it is the union
of ourselves with God.

He who has not forgiven an enemy has never yet tasted
one of the most sublime enjoyments of life.

If pleasure is the highest aim, it will lead to unhappiness.

If you would know sublime happiness, sacrifice pleasure for duty.

In diving to the bottom of pleasures we bring up
more gravel than sand.

Blessed are ye, when men revile you, and persecute you,
and shall say all manner of evil against you falsely, for My sake.
Rejoice and be exceedingly glad; for great is your reward
in heaven: for so persecuted they the prophets
which were before you.

The fear of the Lord makes a merry heart, and gives joy
and gladness, and a long life.

Let those that put their trust in God rejoice: let them ever shout for joy because God defends them.

Many are on the wrong scent in the pursuit of happiness.

Sing your song and your whole heart will be in the singing.

Whoso trusts in the Lord, happy is he.

Cheerfulness is health;
Melancholy is disease.

The best are not only the happiest, but the happiest are usually the best.

A good thing to remember
And a better thing to do
To work with the construction gang
And not with the wrecking crew.

My job is never work—the only time it seems like work is when I'd rather be doing something else.

The purest pleasures are found in useful work.

To love the All-perfect is happiness.

Cheerfulness is the daughter of employment.

Occupation is the necessary basis of all enjoyment.

Sorrow's best antidote is employment.

Wealth is not his that has it, but his that enjoys it.

The covetous man pines in plenty.

God loves a cheerful giver.

What sweet delight a quiet wife affords!

A wife doubles a man's pleasures and divides his cares.

Heaviness in the heart of man makes it stoop; but a good word
makes it glad.

All things are not profitable for all men, neither has every soul
pleasure in everything.

Man should eat and drink and enjoy the good of all his labor;
it is the gift of God.

Happiness or unhappiness depends more on the way we meet events than on the nature of those events themselves.

All heaven is interested in the happiness of man.

We cannot be happy unless we think we are the means of good to others.

The hatred we bear our enemies injures their happiness less than our own.

Dig a man out of trouble, and the hole that is made is the grave for your own sorrows.

Not just live and let live, but live and help live.

Happy is the man that findeth wisdom,
and the man that getteth understanding:
For the merchandise of it is better than
the merchandise of silver, and the gain
thereof than fine gold.
She is more precious than rubies: and
all the things thou canst desire are not to
be compared to her.
Length of days is in her right hand; and
in her left hand riches and honor.

Her ways are ways of pleasantness, and
all her paths are peace.
She is a tree of life to them that lay
hold upon her: and happy is every one that
retaineth her.

They that sow in tears shall reap in joy.

There are no riches above a sound body, and no joy
above the joy of the heart.

Love your own soul, and comfort you heart, remove sorrow from you:
for sorrow has killed many, and there is not profit therein.

Weeping may endure for a night, but joy comes in the morning.

A merry heart does good like a medicine: but a broken spirit
dries the bones.

Pleasant words are as a honeycomb, sweet to the soul,
and health to the bones.

Health makes you feel now is the best time of the year.

Unhappiness is not knowing what we want
and killing ourselves to get it.

Some pleasures are more trouble than trouble.

Happiness is enhanced by others but does not depend
upon others.

He enjoys much who is thankful for little.

O satisfy us early with Thy mercy; that we may rejoice
and be glad all our days.

Happiness is not a reward—it is a consequence.

When you have thanked the Lord for every blessing sent,
but little time will then remain for murmur or lament.

Your joy of the Lord is your strength.

In the world you shall have tribulation, but be of good cheer.

He that is of a merry heart has a continual feast.

Live joyfully with the wife whom thou lovest
all the days of the life of thy vanity . . .
for that is thy portion in this life,
and in thy labor . . . under the sun.

To be happy at home is the ultimate aim of all ambition.

He is happiest who finds his peace in his home.

A man travels the world over in search of what he needs
and returns home to find it.

Activity and sadness are incompatible.

A life of pleasure can be the most sorrowful life.

The flower that follows the sun does so even in cloudy days.

O for the good old days when I was so unhappy.

A sorrow shared is a sorrow halved.

Remember there are no bad day—
some are just better than others.

A child of God should be a visible beatitude of joy and happiness
and a living doxology for gratitude and adoration.

It is good to let a little sunshine out as well as in.

Don't spend your days stringing and tuning your instrument—
start making music now.

A link of man's mind may be forged
by the heart of a song.

A humorist is a man who feels bad, but feels good about it.

How tasteless are the passing pleasures of this world!

Happy is that people whose God is the Lord.

He that loves wisdom loves life; and they that seek her early
shall be filled with joy.

Count it all joy when you fall into sundry temptations, for the trial
of your faith brings forth patience.

If ignorance is bliss, why aren't more people jumping up
and down for joy?

The principal business of life is to enjoy it.

Do not put off until tomorrow
what can be enjoyed today.

Be glad in the Lord, and rejoice, ye righteous: and shout for joy,
all ye that are upright in heart.

O happy day that fixed my choice on Thee my Savior
and my God. Well may this glowing heart rejoice
and tell its rapture all abroad.

Rejoice in the Lord always and again I say, rejoice.

The spirit of melancholy would often take its flight from us
if only we would take up the song of praise.

Joy is everywhere.

Happiness is never caused by circumstances alone.

I am not fully dressed until I adorn myself with a smile of joy.

We may be sure we are not pleasing God
if we are not happy ourselves.

No thoroughly occupied man was ever yet very miserable.

Labor, if it were not necessary for the existence, would be
indispensable for the happiness of men.

Nothing is pleasure that is not spiced with variety.

I do not believe in doing for pleasure things I do not like to do.

Religion may not keep you from sinning
but it takes the joy out of it.

Joy shall be in heaven over one sinner that repenteth, more than
over ninety and nine just persons which need no repentance.

O for thanksgiving for every heart beat and a song for every breath.

The good things of life are not to be had singly,
but come to us with a mixture; like a schoolboy's holiday,
with a task affixed to the tail of it.

Life would be tolerably agreeable
if it were not for its amusements.

The fruit derived from labor is the sweetest of pleasures.

I shall not be gloomy as long as the sun shines.

A man of meditation is happy, not for an hour, or a day, but quite
round the circle of his years.

The foolish man seeks happiness in the distance;
the wise man grows it under his feet.

A cheerful friend is like a sunny day.

Smile for the joy of others.

Delight yourself in the Lord; and He shall give you
the desires of your heart.

The prayer of the upright is God's delight.

PEACE

The Lord is my shepherd;
I shall not want.
He maketh me to lie down in green pastures:
He leadeth me beside the still waters.
He restoreth my soul:
He leadeth me in the paths of righteousness
for His name's sake.
Yea, though I walk through the valley
of the shadow of death,
I will fear no evil: for Thou art with me;
Thy rod and Thy staff they comfort me.
Thou preparest a table before me
in the presence of mine enemies;
thou anointest my head with oil;
My cup runneth over.
Surely goodness and mercy shall follow me
all the days of my life:
And I will dwell in the house
of the Lord forever.

God is not the author of confusion, but of peace.

Be strong and of good courage; be not afraid, neither be dismayed:
for the Lord your God is with you wherever you go.

Is your soul running as though being pursued, with no opportunity
to rest and feed?

He that loves silver shall not be satisfied with silver; nor he
that loves abundance with increase.

Rest is the sweet sauce of labor.

Watching for riches consumes the flesh, and the care thereof
drives away sleep.

Watching care will not let a man slumber,
as a sore disease breaks sleep.

When you have accomplished your daily task, go to sleep in peace;
God is awake!

I will lay me down in peace and sleep: for Thou, Lord,
only makes me dwell in safety.

If I am at war with myself, I can bring little peace
to my fellow man.

I have learned in whatsoever state I am,
therewith to be content.

All men desire peace; few desire the things that make for peace.

As long as man stands in his own way, everything
seems to be in his way.

Well-arranged time is the surest mark of a well-arranged mind.

I am easy to please but difficult to satisfy.

The thing to put aside for one's old age is all thought of retirement.

Doing nothing is the most tiresome job in the world
because you cannot quit and rest.

The sleep of a laboring man is sweet,
whether he eat little or much;
but the abundance of the rich
will not suffer him to sleep.

I was angry with my friend:
I told my wrath, my wrath did end.
I was angry with my foe;
I hid my wrath, my wrath did grow.

A man's venom poisons himself more than his victim.

Marriage with a good woman is a harbor in the tempest of life;
with a bad woman, it is a tempest in the harbor.

Few things are more bitter than to feel bitter.

The evening of a well-spent life brings its lamp with it.

Work is not the cause—
Rest is not the cure.

Rest not from duty, but find rest in it.

Better is a handful with quietness, than both the hands
full with travail and vexation of spirit.

Consider wherein you agree with your opponent,
rather than wherein you differ.

I'm so accustomed to being tense that when I'm calm I get nervous.

How good and how pleasant it is for brothers
to dwell together in unity.

The Lord is on my side; I will not fear: What can man do unto me?

To be carnally minded is death; but to be spiritually minded
is life and peace.

Think little of what others think of you.

Don't hurry, don't worry,
Do your best, and leave the rest.

If we find not repose in ourselves, it is in vain to seek it elsewhere.

Fear nothing so much as sin.

There is no witness so terrible—no accuser so powerful—
as conscience which dwells within us.

There is no peace, says the Lord, unto the wicked.

If it be possible, as much as lies in you, live peaceably with all men.

Mark the perfect man and behold the upright;
for the end of that man is peace.

Worry—a mental tornado—a dog chasing its own tail.

To carry care to bed is to sleep with a pack on your back.

This is maturity:
To be able to stick with a job until it is finished;
to be able to bear an injustice without wanting to get even;
to be able to carry money without spending it;
and to do one's duty without being supervised.

Godliness with contentment is great gain.

Religion has long been used to comfort the troubled. May it
sometimes be used to trouble the comfortable.

Pure gold can lie for a month in the furnace without losing a grain.

Jesus said: "Come unto Me, all ye that labor and are heavy laden,
and I will give you rest."

Follow after the things that make for peace, and things
where with one may edify another.

Being justified by faith, we have peace with God
through our Lord Jesus Christ.

I shall grow old, but never lose life's zest
Because the road's last turn will be the best.
Expect the best!
It lies not in the past.
God ever keeps the good wine to the last.

Beyond are nobler work and sweeter rest.
Expect the best!

The Lord is my light and my salvation;
whom shall I fear?
The Lord is the strength of my life;
of whom shall I be afraid?

In solitude we are least alone.

I should know myself better if there were not so many of me.

Mercy and truth are met together; righteousness and peace
have kissed each other.

My son, forget not My law;
but let your heart keep My commandments:
for length of days, and long life,
and peace shall they add to you.

How men treat us will make little difference when we know
we have God's approval.

One who is afraid of lying is usually afraid of nothing else.

Be still and know that I am God.

Cast all your care upon God; for He cares for you.

He that dwells in the secret place of the most High
shall abide under the shadow of the Almighty.
I will say of the Lord, He is my refuge and my fortress:
my God, in Him will I trust.
Surely He shall deliver you from the snare of the fowler,
and from the noisome pestilence.
He shall cover you with His feathers,
and under His wings shall you trust:
His truth shall be your shield and buckler.
You shall not be afraid for the terror of night:
nor for the arrow that flies by day

LONG SUFFERING

Great victories come, not through ease but by fighting valiantly
and meeting hardships bravely.

If you can't have the best of everything, make the best
of everything you have.

Patience is the finest and worthiest part of fortitude.

We can do anything we want to if we stick to it long enough.

If you faint in the day of adversity, your strength is small.

The secret of success is constancy to purpose.

Men do not fail; they give up trying.

The grinding that would wear away to nothing a lesser stone,
merely serves to give luster to a diamond.

Sometimes a noble failure serves the world
as faithfully as a distinguished success.

Difficulties strengthen the mind, as labor does the body.

The man who rows the boat doesn't have time to rock it.

Luck means the hardships and privations which you have not
hesitated to endure, the long nights you have devoted to work.
Luck means the appointments you have never failed to keep;
the trains you have never failed to catch.

A little more determination,
A little more pluck,
A little more work—
that's LUCK.

Mastery in any art comes only with long practice.

If at first you do succeed, try something harder.

A fella doesn't last long on what he has done;
he has to keep delivering.

Free enterprise gives everybody a chance to get to the top. Some
depend too much on the free and not enough on the enterprise.

The early bird gets the firm.

Not everyone that says unto Me, Lord, Lord,
shall enter into the kingdom of heaven; but he that does the will
of My Father which is in heaven.

As sure as ever God puts his children in the furnace,
He will be in the furnace with them.

It is not until we have passed through the furnace
that we are made to know how much dross there is
in our composition.

I have fought a good fight, I have finished my course,
I have kept the Faith; henceforth there is laid up for me a crown
of righteousness, which the Lord, the righteous Judge,
shall give me at that day: and not to me only, but unto all them
also that love His appearing.

The grass is greener on the other side,
but it is just as hard to mow.

A smooth sea never made a skillful mariner.

The cloud that darkens the present hour may brighten
all our future days.

It is easier to fight for one's principles than to live up to them.

Life, misfortune, isolation, abandonment, poverty are battlefields, which have their heroes,—heroes obscure, but sometimes greater than those who become illustrations.

Salvation is free, but being Christian is costly.

Shoot at everything and hit nothing.

Making excuses doesn't change the truth.

Could not the victories of the weaker be the greater?

Give wind and tide a chance to change.

The error of youth is to believe that intelligence is a substitute for experience, while the error of age is to believe that experience is a substitute for intelligence.

Judge nothing before the time.

Don't lessen the lesson.

Experience is what makes you wonder how it got a reputation for being the best teacher.

Cast out the beam first of your own eye; and then you shall see
clearly to cast out the mote of your brother's eye.

If I could only see the road you came,
With all the jagged rocks and crooked ways,
I might more kindly think of your misstep
And only praise.

It is difficult to say who does us the most mischief—our enemies
with the worst intentions or our friends with the best.

Many are the afflictions of the righteous; but the Lord
delivers him out of them all.

If I could only know the heartaches you have felt,
The longing for the things that never came,
I would not misconstrue your erring then
Nor ever blame.

All people are born equal. Each has a right to earn his niche
by the sweat of his brow. But some sweat more
and carve larger niches.

Remember there's blue sky behind the blackest cloud.

When you begin to coast you know you're on the downgrade.

You that fear the Lord, wait for His mercy;
and go not aside, lest you fall.

If your cup seems too bitter, if your burden seems too heavy, be sure
that it is the wounded hand that is holding the cup, and that it is He
who carries the cross that is carrying the burden.

God will not look you over for medals, degrees, or diplomas,
but for scars.

Our light affliction, which is but for a moment, works for us a far
more exceeding and eternal weight of glory.

The sufferings of this present time are not worthy to be compared
with the glory which shall be revealed in us.

The dictionary is the only place success comes before work.

Set your heart aright, constantly endure, and make not haste
in time of trouble.

It is better to wear out than to rust out.

Trouble and perplexity drive me to prayer, and prayer drives away
perplexity and trouble.

Better to limp all the way to heaven than not get there at all.

Sanctified afflictions are spiritual promotions.

He surely is most in need of another's patience,
who has none of his own.

They also serve who only stand and wait.

Wait on the Lord: be of good courage, and He shall strengthen
your heart: wait, I say, on the Lord.

They that wait upon the Lord shall renew their strength;
they shall mount up with wings as eagles; they shall run,
and not be weary; and they shall walk, and not faint.

Parents who wish to train their children in the way they should go,
must go in the way which they would have their children go.

The most generous vine, if not pruned,
runs out into many superfluous stems and grows at last weak
and fruitless; so does the best man if he be not cut short
in his desires and pruned afflictions.

In youth we run into difficulties;
in age difficulties run into us.

Young men these days seem to confuse starting at the bottom
with getting in on the ground floor.

God sometimes washes the eyes of His children
with tears, that they may read aright His providence
and His commandments.

Sometimes, when all life's lessons have been learned . . . we shall
see how all God's plans were right, and how what seemed reproof
was love most true.

Patience is not passive; on the contrary, it is active;
it is concentrated strength.

Anytime a man takes a stand, there'll come a time when he'll
be tested to see how firm his feet are planted.

You and I cannot determine what other men shall think
and say about us. We can only determine what they ought to think
of us and say about us.

You can tell some people aren't afraid of work
by the way they fight it.

Toil awhile, endure awhile, believe always,
and never turn back.

Adversity is the only balance to weigh friends—
prosperity is no just scale.

God will not suffer you to be tempted above that you are able;
but will with the temptation also make a way to escape,
that ye may be able to bear it.

Christianity has not been tried and found wanting; it has been found
difficult and not tried.

Fundamentally true ideas possess greater ultimate power
than physical might.

You can't slide uphill.

Men are apt to settle a question rightly when it is discussed freely.

People do not lack strength; they lack will.

The quitter never wins.
The winner never quits.

Be no more by a storm dismayed,
for by it the full-grown seeds are laid;
And though the tree by its might it shatters,
What then, if thousands of seeds it scatters?

Life is never so bad at its worst
that it is impossible to live;
it is never so good at its best
that it is easy to live.

Borrowing trouble from the future does not deplete the supply.

Living the good life is not a fair weather job.

Make the most of the best and the least of the worst.

Troubles are often the tools by which God fashions us
for better things.

Never despair, but if you do, work on in despair.

In great attempts it is glorious even to fail.

It is by those who have suffered that the world is most advanced.

If we were faultless we should not be so much annoyed
by the defects of others.

Speakers have been showering us with pearls of wisdom for centuries,
and if their valuable advice were laid end to end, it would still be just
as good as new. Very little of it has ever been used.

If you are not able to make yourself what you wish, how can you expect to mold another to your will?

The way of the world is to praise dead saints and persecute living ones.

Temperament is temper that is too old to spank.

Building boys is easier than mending men.

It is the practice of the multitude to bark at eminent men as little dogs at strangers.

Understanding is the secret of withstanding.

If a man empties his purse into his head, no man can take it from him.

No one agrees with the opinions of others. He merely agrees with his own opinions expressed by somebody else.

An obstinate man does not hold opinions—they hold him.

He that has no cross will have no crown.

The greatest affliction of life is never to be afflicted.

Carry your cross patiently and with perfect submission,
and in the end it shall carry you.

A just man falls seven times, and rises up again.

What man calls fortune is from God.

A purpose is the eternal condition of success.

Though our outward man perish, yet the inward man
is renewed day by day.

Fret not thyself because of evil men,
neither be envious at the wicked;
for there shall be no reward to the evil man;
the candle of the wicked shall be put out.

That which is painful to the body may be
profitable to the soul.

Good timber does not grow in ease,
The stronger wind, the stronger trees;
The farther sky the greater length,
The more the storms the more the strength.
By sun and cold, by rain and snow,
In tree or man good timber grows.

Patience is bitter, but its fruit is sweet.

Instruction may end in the schoolroom, but education
ends only with life.

There are those who are ever learning and never able to come
to the knowledge of the truth.

Talent knows what to do; tact knows when
and how to do it.

Poise is the art of raising the eyebrows instead of the roof.

Character development is the true aim of education.

An ounce of pluck is worth a ton of luck.

The same furnace that liquefies the gold hardens the clay.

The worst men often give the best advice.

Nothing is done finally and right. Nothing is known positively
and completely.

The late blooming virtues can be the very best.

Confront improper conduct, not by retaliation,
but by example.

Firmness is that admirable quality in ourselves that is merely
stubbornness in others.

Whosoever will save his life shall lose it; and whosoever shall
lose his life for My sake shall find it.

He conquers who endures.

Let those who suffer according to the will of God commit the keeping
of their souls to Him in well doing, as unto a faithful Creator.

As threshing separates the wheat from the chaff,
so does affliction purify virtue.

Be not overcome of evil, but overcome evil with good.

Idleness is the burial of a living person.

Recreation is not being idle; it is easing the wearied part
by change of occupation.

The clock of life is wound but once,
And no man has the power to tell

Just when the hands will stop
At late or early hour.
Now is the only time you own:
Live, love toil with a will,
Place no faith in tomorrow;
For the clock may then be still.

The virtue lies in the struggle, not in the prize.

GENTLENESS

We cannot always oblige, but we can always speak obligingly.

Wouldn't it be nice if we could find other things
as easily as we find fault?

A word of kindness is seldom spoken in vain,
while witty sayings are easily lost as the pearls
slipping from a broken string.

No man has it so good but that two or three words can dishearten,
and there is no calamity but a few right words can hearten.

Speak not evil one of another.

To listen well is as to talk well and is as essential
to all true conversation.

Speak gently—it is better far to rule by love than fear. Speak gently—
let no harsh words mar the good we might do here.

Diplomacy is to do and say the nastiest thing
in the nicest way.

Let the words of my mouth and the meditation of my heart
be always acceptable in Thy sight, O Lord, my strength
and my Redeemer.

The greatest truths are the simplest; and so are the greatest men.

A small unkindness is a great offense.

I have wept in the night for the shortness of sight
That to somebody's need made me blind;
But I never have yet felt a twinge of regret
For being a little too kind.

As we have opportunity, let us do good unto all men.

Be careful how you live; you may be the only Bible
some people read.

The servant of the Lord must not strive, but be gentle
unto all men, apt to teach, patient, in meekness instructing
those who oppose themselves.

The milk of human kindness never curdles.

Man's inhumanity to man makes countless thousands mourn.

Be kind, one to another, tenderhearted, forgiving one another, even as God for Christ's sake has forgiven you.

Good manners are the small coin of virtue.

He who reforms himself has done much toward reforming others.

Bless them that persecute you.

Rejoice with them that do rejoice and weep with them that weep.

Be not forgetful to entertain strangers: for thereby some have entertained angels unawares.

Today's profits are yesterday's goodwill ripened.

A good name is rather to be chosen than great riches, and loving favor rather than silver and gold.

To belittle is to be little.

Let me grow lovely, growing old—
So many fine things do:

Lace and ivory and gold
And silks need not be new.
There is healing in old trees,
Old streets a glamour hold.
Why may not I, as well as these,
Grow lovely, growing old.

One who grimly declares, "I shall do my duty,"
is facing a drab experience. A smile and kindly
understanding can generate warmth
to melt the grimness and compulsion.

A noble heart, like the sun, shows its greatest countenance
in its lowest estate.

The wisdom that is from above is first pure, then peaceable,
gentle, and easy to be entreated, full of mercy and good fruits,
without partiality, and without hypocrisy.

What we need is not new light, but new sight;
not new paths, but new strength to walk in the old ones;
not new duties but new strength from on High to fulfill those
that are plain before us.

Punctuality is the politeness of kings and the duty
of gentle people everywhere.

True politeness is perfect ease and freedom; it simply consists in treating others just as you love to be treated yourself.

It is they who do their duties in every-day and trivial matters who fulfill them on great occasions.

It is only imperfection that is intolerant of what is imperfect. The more perfect we are, the more gentle and quiet we become toward the defects of others.

It isn't so much what's on the table that matters but what's on the chairs.

Be of the same mind one toward another. Mind not high things but condescend to men of low estate.

A rolling stone gathers no moss but it obtains a certain polish.

Culture is one thing and varnish another.

The habit of expressing appreciation is oil on troubled waters. It is the essence of graciousness, kindness, and fair dealing. Fortunately, it is a habit that can be formed by anyone who will take the trouble.

What you dislike in another, take care to correct in yourself.

Manners are minor morals.

A little more tired at the close of the day,
A little less anxious to have our way,
A little less anxious to scold and blame,
A little more care for a brother's name;
And so we are nearing the journey's end,
Where time and eternity meet and blend.

A soft answer turns away wrath, but grievous words stir up anger.

A real friend is one who helps us to think our noblest thoughts,
put forth our best efforts, and to be our best selves.

GOODNESS

For kindness is indeed sublime and worth the trouble anytime.
Sincerity is all we need to help us do a friendly deed.

Give to him that asks you; from him that would borrow
of you turn not away.

As you would that men should do to you,
do also to them likewise.

Be great in act, as you have been in thought. Suit the action
to the word and the word to the action.

No man can be good to others without being good to himself.

Our deeds determine us as much as we determine our deeds.

The rung of a ladder was never meant to rest upon,
but only to hold a man's foot long enough to enable him
to put the other one higher.

Judge not, and you shall not be judged: condemn not, and you shall not be condemned: forgive, and you shall be forgiven.

Jesus went about doing good.

Whatever makes good Christians makes them good citizens.

The hand that's dirty with honest labor is fit
to shake with any neighbor.

To him that knows to do good, and does it not,
to him it is sin.

Can my creed be recognized in my deed?

The goodness of God endures continually.

The good-natured person is described in one of Paul's letters—
"envieth not—not puffed up—not easily provoked—seeketh no evil."
To sum it up, his nature is GOOD.

Be not weary in well doing; for in due season you shall reap,
if you faint not.

He who masters his words will master his works.

Not the hearers of the law are just before God, but the doers of the law shall be justified.

Man looks on the outward appearance; but God looks on the heart.

The man who is mean is meaner to himself than anyone else.

Abhor that which is evil; cleave to that which is good.

We persuade others by being in earnest ourselves.

Be what you say and say what you are.

Let word, creed, and deed be integrated in one truth.

Honesty is always the best policy.

A problem honestly stated is half solved.

No man has good enough memory to make a successful liar.

Truth cannot be killed with the sword nor abolished by law.

It is better to suffer for speaking the truth than that the truth should suffer for want of speaking it.

Truth is not only violated by falsehood; it may be equally outraged by silence.

It is easy to tell a lie; but hard to tell only one lie.

If we ever have a golden age, it will be because golden hearts are beating in it.

Character is a diamond that scratches every other stone.

There is no liberty in wrong-doing.

It is difficult to believe in the goodness of disagreeable people.

God listens to our hearts, rather than to our lips.

Better is a little with righteousness than great revenues without right.

Money dishonestly acquired is never worth its cost, while a good conscience never costs as much as it is worth.

Prefer loss before unjust gain.

O, what a tangled web we weave, when first we practice to deceive.

Discover what is true and practice what is good.

No service is too small and none is too great,
from the giving of a cup of cold water
to the laying down of one's life.

Many faults in our neighbor should be of less consequence to us
than one of the smallest in ourselves.

If you follow righteousness, you shall obtain her and put her on
as a glorious long robe.

No man has a right to do as he pleases, except when he pleases
to do right.

Nothing can be truly great that is not right.

Everything great is not always good, but all good things are great.

When we snub, we snub Christ;
When we neglect, we neglect Christ;
When we hate, we hate Christ.
Wherever we turn, there is Christ in one
of our brothers to bless or to hurt.

He that abides in Me, and I in him,
the same brings forth much fruit:
for without Me you can do nothing.

He that does good for good's sake seeks neither praise nor reward,
but he is sure of both in the end.

Life is a steep grade, and we should welcome every opportunity
to give our friends a lift when they need it.

There may be times when you cannot find help, but there is no time
when you cannot give help.

Do good with what you have, or it will do you no good.

If you do what you should not, you must bear what you would not.

We reform others unconsciously when we walk uprightly.

Prove all things; hold fast that which is good.

Act as if each day were given you for Christmas, just as eager,
just as proud!

Help your brother's boat across, and lo! your own has reached the shore.

He is greatest who is most useful to others.

Whatever is worth doing at all, is worth doing well.

Good thoughts are little better than good dreams
except they be put in action.

Practice an attitude of gratitude.

What you are thunders so loud I cannot hear what you say.

He who wishes to secure the good of others
has already secured his own.

There is so much good in the worst of us, and so much bad in the best
of us, that it behooves all of us not to talk about the rest of us.

If the cake is bad, what good is the frosting?

At doing what we shouldn't we are all experts!

From the errors of others a wise man corrects his own.

To err is human; to forgive divine.

Legal immunity does not confer moral immunity.

The prodigal robs his heir; the miser robs himself.

To be good is fine, but to be proud of it ruins the whole thing.

Whosoever shall compel you to go a mile, go with him two.

Whosoever shall smite you on your right cheek,
turn to him the other also.

A good man leaves a good legacy if he leaves his children educated.

The naked truth is not indecent.

The study of God's word, for the purpose of discovering God's will,
is the secret discipline that has formed the greatest characters.

Whatsoever things are true,
Whatsoever things are honest,
Whatsoever things are just,
Whatsoever things are pure,
Whatsoever things are lovely,
Whatsoever things are of good report,
If there be any virtue,
If there be any praise,
Think on these things.

FAITH

Faith is the substance of things hoped for, the evidence
of things not seen.

I know not what the future holds, but I know Who holds the future.

Some men have many reasons why they cannot do what they want,
when all they need is one reason why they can.

The trial of your faith is more precious than gold.

Earnestly contend for the faith that was once delivered
to the saints.

The blind with their hand in God's, can see more clearly
than those who can see who have no faith.

Never put a question mark where God puts a period.

Faith is the awareness of utter helplessness without God.

Know this that the trying of your faith works patience.
Let patience have her perfect work, that you may be perfect
and entire, wanting nothing.

Use your gifts faithfully, and they shall be enlarged; practice what you
know, and you shall attain to higher knowledge.

Have faith in the force of right and not the right of force.

Only you can do it, but you can't do it alone.

The word disappointment is not in the Dictionary of Faith.

All unbelief is the belief of a lie.

Sometimes faith must learn a deeper rest.

Faith grows in the valley.

Faith and work are twins.

Faith is the victory that overcomes the world.

The well of Providence is deep.
It's the buckets we bring to it that are small.

Take one step toward God, and He will take two steps
toward you.

Faith does not exclude work, but only the merit of work.

The end of our faith is the salvation of our souls.

Christianity regulates the whole man in all departments
of his existence.

God is only a prayer away.

Our grand business in life is not to see what lies dimly
at a distance, but to do what lies clearly at hand.

The horizon is not the boundary of the world.

The things that are seen are temporal, but the things
that are not seen are eternal.

He that believes on the Son has everlasting life.

Be persuaded that, what He has promised,
He is able also to perform.

All efforts to destroy are vain—
God's Holy Word will still remain;
So hammer on, ye hostile hands,
Your hammers break, God's anvil stands.

Prayer is the key in the hand of the faith that unlocks
heaven's storehouse.

Men do not need to be instructed how to pray in the midst of battle.

Except the Lord build the house, they labor in vain that build it;
except the Lord keep the city, the watchman wakes but in vain.

A man is not justified by the works of the law, but by the faith
of Jesus Christ.

Even if you knew how much time I spend on my knees
you do not know how much I pray.

God cares not for much prayers but good prayers.

Reach out the hand of faith and touch the throttle of prayer.

The prayer of faith shall save the sick, and the Lord
shall raise him up.

Should Thy mercy send me sorrow, toil, and woe,
Or should pain attend me on my path below;
Grant that I may never fail Thy hand to see;
Grant that I may ever cast my care on Thee.

By grace are you saved through faith; and that not of yourselves: it is
the gift of God—not of works lest man should boast.

The Bible is a surer and safer guide through life
than human reason.

Faith does not spring out of feeling but feeling out of faith. The less
we feel the more we should trust.

No cloud can overshadow a true Christian, but his faith
will discern a rainbow in it.

The real victory of Faith is to trust God in the dark.

If a man could have his wishes, he would double his troubles.

If you have faith as a grain of mustard seed, nothing
shall be impossible unto you.

Ask in faith, nothing wavering. For he that wavers is like a wave
of the sea driven with the wind and tossed.

Trust in the Lord, and do good; so shall you dwell in the land,
and verily you shall be fed.

Youth and Age look upon life from the opposite ends
of the telescope; to the one it is exceedingly long, to the other
exceedingly short.

It is impossible that anything so natural, so necessary, and so universal
as death should ever have been designed as an evil to mankind.

Teach me to live that I may dread the grave as little as my bed.

Draw near to God, and He will draw to you.

God did not remove the Red Sea, and He will lead us through our
difficulties if they cannot be removed.

We walk by faith, not by sight.

Whatever He sends, whether sunshine or dew, is needed for your
soul's health.

Take no thought for your life, what you shall eat; neither
for your body, what you shall put on. The life is more than meat,
and the body is more than raiment.

The Bible is a mirror in which man sees himself as he is.

Faith comes by hearing, and hearing by the word of God.

Faith takes God at His word whatever He says.

Consider the lilies of the field, how they grow; they toil not,
neither do they spin, yet I say unto you that Solomon
in all his glory was not arrayed like one of these.

All else fail—Thou dost not fail! I rest upon Thy word alone.

I am the bread of life: he that come to Me shall never hunger;
and he that believes in Me shall never thirst.

Our strength lies in our dependence on God.

Work is faith made perfect.

He gives the very best to those who leave the choice with Him.

The test of our faith is our eagerness to proclaim the good news.

I am the way, the truth, and the life:
No man comes unto the Father but by me.

You are coming to the King—
Large petitions with you bring—
For His grace and power are such—
None can ever ask too much.

The sheep in the Shepherd's arm looks only into the face
of the Shepherd and not to the wolves nearby
seeking to harm him.

Trust in the Lord with all your heart; and lean not unto
your own understanding.

Examine yourselves, whether you be in the faith;
prove your own selves.

No one is safe who does not learn to trust God for everything.

You have not, because you ask not.

Stagger not at the promise of God through unbelief; but be strong
in faith, giving glory to God.

A ship is safest in deep water.

Fear God, and we shall have no need to fear Adam
or the atom.

You turn to God when storm clouds brew,
And pray to Him for light;
Would you know all God's good for you,
Try praying when the skies are bright.

Never think that God's delays are God's denials.

True prayer always receives what is asked or something better.

Faith is the eyesight of the soul.

Here, believe.
There, understand.

Nothing is or can be accidental with God.

God will supply, but we must apply.

The effectual, fervent prayer of a righteous man avails much.

There are moments when whatever be the attitude of the body,
the soul is on its knees.

God is able to do exceeding abundantly above all that we ask
or think, according to the power that works in us.

The law of prayer is more powerful and just as universal
as the law of gravity.

Our prayer is the sum of our duty. Ask God for what we need
and watch and labor for all that we ask.

Whatever we beg of God, let us also work for it.

Pray our work and work our prayers.

By trials, God is shaping us for higher things. We are always
in the forge or on the anvil.

If God be for us, who can be against us?

How calmly may we commend ourselves to the hands
of Him Who bears up the world.

Continue in prayer, and watch in the same with thanksgiving.

O Lord, open Thou my lips and my mouth shall show forth
Thy praise.

Are we loaded down with an inadequate religion, rather than
being lifted up with a faith that really sustains?

A weak man becomes powerful when he is in contact
with the mighty forces of God.

The gospel of Christ is the power of God unto salvation
to everyone that believes.

Believe in God, and He will help you; order your way aright,
and trust in Him.

The just shall live by faith.

Launch out into the deep—let the shoreline go.

The outlook may be dark, but the uplook is glorious.

MEEKNESS

Humble yourselves in the sight of the Lord, and He shall lift you up.

Not many of us are material for greatness, according to the general acceptance of the term, but each has something to give to justify the gift of life. The humblest can become kindly and easy to live with.

The meek will He guide in judgment: and the meek
will He teach His way.

True greatness consists in being great in little things.

What one is in little things he is also in great.

A small leak will sink a great ship.

It is easy to dodge an elephant but not a fly.

God has two dwellings: one in heaven and the other
in a meek and thankful heart.

A modest man ever shuns making himself the subject
of his conversation.

Pride makes us esteem ourselves; vanity desires the esteem of others.

Give many men your ear but few your voice.

Though the Lord be high; yet has He respect unto the lowly.

Be subject one to another, and be clothed with humility; for God
resists the proud and gives grace to the humble.

Be sure of this: You are dreadfully like other people.

The greater we are, the more humble we are.

Think not of yourself more highly than you ought to think.

May I remember that mankind got along very well before my birth
and in all probability will get along very well after my death.

Whosoever shall exalt himself shall be abased; and he that shall
humble himself shall be exalted.

A good penny is better than a bad nickel.

Humility is only gratitude.

To accept good advice is but to increase one's own ability.

Humility is the solid foundation of all the virtues.

He who glories, let him glory in the Lord.

He that is warned by the folly of others has perhaps attained
the soundest wisdom.

Knowledge makes men humble, and true genius is ever modest.

Be not like the cock who thought the sun rose to hear him crow.

We may learn silence from the talkative, toleration from the
intolerant, kindness from the unkind.

Speak as to be only the arrow in the bow that the Almighty draws.

No person can ever be a complete failure, for he may serve
as a horrible example.

The man who leaves home to set the world on fire
often comes back for more matches.

May we all be praying publicans lest we should become
self-righteous Pharisees.

Self-satisfaction dulls the ambition and blunts the scent for opportunity. Its frequent companions are selfishness, snobbery, and indolence.

The prayer of the humble pierces the clouds.

When you think you stand, take heed lest you fall.

Who can number the sand of the sea,
and the drops of rain,
and the days of eternity?

The gliding of the key will not make it open
the door better.

Seek not out the things that are too hard for you, neither search the things that are above your strength.

When you pray, enter into your closet, and when you have shut the door, pray to your Father which is in secret; and your Father which sees in secret shall reward you openly.

What if the little rain should say,
"As small a drop as I
Can never refresh a drooping earth,
I'll tarry in the sky."

The beginning of pride is when one departs from God, and his heart is turned away from his maker.

Who has deceived you so often as yourself?

Meekness is not weakness.

Meekness is surrendering to God.

Nothing will make us so charitable and tender to the faults of others as to thoroughly examine ourselves.

Pride goes before destruction, and a haughty spirit before a fall.

It is of no advantage for man to know much unless he lives according to what he knows.

Talk to a man about himself, and he will listen for hours.

Snobs talk as if they had begotten their ancestors.

If the whole world followed you,
Followed to the letter,
Tell me—if it followed you,
Would the world be better?

Exalt not yourself lest you fall.

Faith and meekness are a delight to God.

People put a low estimate on the man who puts
too high an estimate on himself.

You can always spot a well-informed man—
his views are the same as yours.

Who can understand his errors?
Cleanse Thou me from secret faults.

If you were to list the ten smartest people,
who would be the other nine?

God speaks to man when man admits he has absolutely nothing to say.

Before honor is humility.

Walk worthy of the vocation wherewith you are called, with all
lowliness and meekness, with long suffering, forbearing one another in
love, endeavoring to keep the unity of the Spirit in the bond of peace.

There is more hope of a fool than of a man wise in his own conceit.

He tried to be somebody by trying to be like everybody,
which makes him a nobody.

If the best man's faults were written on his forehead, he would draw
his hat over his eyes.

Some men never feel small, but these are the few men who are.

Better to speak wisdom foolishly than to speak folly wisely.

A child can ask many questions the wisest man cannot answer.

We may be taught by every person we meet.

Seeing ourselves as others see us wouldn't do much good—we
wouldn't believe it anyway.

Man shall ever stand in need of man.

Who is like unto the Lord our God, Who dwells on high,
Who humbles Himself to behold the things that are in Heaven,
and in the earth.

If my people, which are called by My name, shall humble themselves,
and pray, and seek My face, and turn from their wicked ways; then will
I hear from heaven, and will forgive their sin, and will heal their land.

Humility is that low sweet root, from which all
heavenly virtues shoot.

Receive with meekness the engrafted Word, which is able
to save your souls.

The wisdom of this world is foolishness with God.

Do the truth you know, and you shall learn the truth
you need to know.

If you have knowledge let others light their candles by it.

He that swells in prosperity will be sure to shrink in poverty.

Blessed are the meek, for they shall inherit the earth.

TEMPERANCE

No man is free who cannot command himself.

I always think before I speak.
I find this rather balking,
For by the time my thinking's done,
Somebody else is talking.

Think all you speak, but speak not all you think.

Let your speech be short, comprehending much in few words;
be as one that knows and yet holds his tongue.

Brevity is the soul of wit and even wit is a burden
when it talks too long.

A wholesome tongue is a tree of life.

A good listener is not only popular everywhere,
but after a while he knows something.

Silence is one of the great arts of conversation.

Nothing is opened more by mistake than the mouth.

In the multitude of words there wants no sin;
but he that refrains his lips is wise.

If any man offend not in word, the same is a perfect man
and able also to bridle the whole body.

Every idle word that men shall speak, they shall give account
thereof in the day of judgment.

Let no corrupt communication proceed out of your mouth;
but that which is good to the use of edifying.

Death and life are in the power of the tongue.

Habit is either the best of servants or the worst of masters.

We first make our habits, and then our habits make us.

Habits are at first cobwebs, then cables.

Even a fool, when he holds his peace, is counted wise:
and he that shuts his lips is esteemed a man of understanding.

They think too little who talk too much.

The chains of habit are generally too small to be felt
until they are too strong to be broken.

It is the neglect of timely repair that makes rebuilding necessary.

We perform many acts automatically. We have formed
the habit of walking, eating, etc., without
conscious thought. In the moral realm, we can so form
the habit of living up to our better selves
that this also becomes automatic.

When a good man has not a good reason for doing a thing,
he has one good reason for letting it alone.

Be sober, be vigilant; because your adversary the devil, as a
roaring lion, walks about, seeking whom he may devour.

Being overly careful about tiny details of one virtue can't make up
for complete neglect of another duty.

Moderation in temper is a virtue. Moderation
in principle is a vice.

A tree will not only lay as it falls, but it will fall as it leans.

Lord, so teach us to number our days that we may apply
our hearts unto wisdom.

No gain is so certain as that which proceeds from the economical
use of what you already have.

If you know how to spend less than you get, you have the
philosopher's tone.

Prosperity's right hand is industry, and her left hand is frugality.

Some people wait to start saving for a rainy day until
it starts sprinkling.

A man is rich in proportion to the number of things
that he can afford to let alone.

The safest way to double your money is to fold it over once
and put it in your pocket.

Economy is in itself a source of great revenue.

The saving of money usually means the saving of man. It means
cutting off indulgences or avoiding vicious habits.

Money is a good servant, but a poor master.

A penny saved is as good as a penny earned.

Riches are not an end of life, but an instrument of life.

He is rich whose income is more than his expenses; he is poor whose expenses exceed his income.

What does the man want who has enough?

Leisure for men of business and business for men of leisure would cure many complaints.

Good luck is a lazy man's estimate of a worker's success.

He is already poverty-stricken whose habits are not thrifty.

Gold has been the ruin of many.

Waste not, want not.

Willful waste makes woeful want.

The man who does nothing but wait for his ship to come in has already missed the boat.

Can a man take fire in his bosom, and his clothes not be burned? Can one go upon hot coals, and his feet not be burned?

Hard work is an accumulation of easy things you didn't do when you should have.

Make your recreation servant to your business, lest you become a servant to your recreation.

Waste of time is the most extravagant and costly of all expenses.

Leisure is a beautiful garment, but it will not do for constant wear.

"The longest way around is the shortest way home." "Make haste slowly." "Haste makes waste." These are all homely proverbs with the same meaning; namely, careful painstaking effort pays in the long run.

When angry, count ten before you speak; if very angry, count a hundred.

Anger, if not restrained, is frequently more hurtful to us than the injury that provokes it.

Temper, if ungoverned, governs the whole man.

He who can suppress a moment's anger
may prevent a day of sorrow.

It is not what people eat, but what they digest,
that makes them strong. It is not what they gain, but what they save,
that makes them rich. It is not what they read, but what
they remember, that makes them learn.

Regret is an appalling waste of energy; you can't build on it;
it is only good for wallowing in.

There are times when nothing a man can say
is nearly so powerful as saying nothing.

A stitch in time saves nine.

A covetous man's eye is not satisfied with his portion.

The key to a lot of troubles is the one that fits the ignition.

Statistics prove folks who drive like crazy are.

He who feasts every day feasts no day.

It is never safe to consider individuals in groups, classes,
or races. To ascribe virtues or vices to all the individuals of a group
is as senseless as it is unjust and inaccurate.

The ally of tolerance is knowledge.
As a rule, understanding of another's nature
precludes hostility. This holds good between nations and races,
as well as between individuals.

The excess of our youth are drafts upon our old age, payable,
with interest, about thirty years after date.

Folk who never do more than they get paid for seldom get paid
for more than they do.

Some live without working
and others work without living.

He is not poor who has little, but he that desires much.

The first step in making a dream come true is to wake up.

Thrift is essential to well-ordered living.

Wealth is a means to an end and not the end itself.

He who has little and wants less is richer than he who has much and wants more.

A spender's solvency depends more upon his attitude than upon his income.

He is richest who is content with the least.

He that buys what he does not want will soon want what he cannot buy.

Many would never know want had they not first known waste.

Choose rather to want less than to have more.

There would not be so many open mouths if there were not so many open ears.

Discretion in speech is more than eloquence.

Gossip is putting 2 and 2 together and making 5.

How many friends would remain if all persons knew what each said of the other?

A prudent wife is from the Lord.

Every wise woman builds her own house: but the foolish
plucks it down with her hands.

Herein are great rules of life contracted into short sentences
that may be easily impressed on the memory
and so recur habitually to the mind.

TREASURES OF SILVER

LOVE • JOY • PATIENCE
MEEKNESS • GOODNESS • INNER PEACE

LOVE

Life without love would be like the earth without the sun.

Love is the greatest thing in the world!

Jesus loves the little children
All the children of the world—
Red and yellow, black and white,
All are precious in His sight.

Everyone of us is the object of God's care as though we were
the only one in the world.

God does not play favorites.

Jesus loves me, this I know
For the BIBLE tells me so!

No person is outside the scope of God's love.

When God said "whosoever," He included me!

God loved us so much that He sent His Son, Jesus, to earth
to show us the way to heaven.

God's love will meet my every need.

I could talk forever
Of Jesus' love divine—
Of all His care and tenderness
For your life and for mine.

All lovers are but a reflection of God's love for us.

I love God because He first loved me.

If I truly love God, I shall love all others.

To live above with saints we love
O friend, that will be glory.
To live below with saints we know
Is quite a different story.

God loves me in spite of my faults.

I should love others in spite of their faults.

If I love, I love God.

Where love is, there God is.

Love behaves.

If I love Jesus, I will do what He says.

Heaven and earth shall some day pass away, but not Jesus' words.

If I love you I will not lie to you nor about you.

If I love my parents, I will honor them and do nothing
to make them unhappy.

If I love the poor, I will give to them.

I must even love my enemies.

I must love one who says bad about me.

If I remember to do Jesus' words, I shall know the truth
and the truth will make me free.

Love doesn't think bad things.

Love does not get angry easily.

Love doesn't brag about me.

Love God and all things will work together for good.

We love when it makes us happier for the other person to be happy than to be happy ourselves.

Love loves to help another.

He who does not love does not know God for God is love.

We owe our love to every person because God made every person and God loves every person.

If I love, that takes care of everything.

Now if I love like this, I know God's love is in me, for my love would not be that loving.

If I love, then I know God lives inside me.

Love praises others.

Love puts up with an awful lot.

Love is funny—the more you give away
the more you seem to have left.

Love doesn't get tired.

Love outlasts everything else.

The worst kind of heart trouble is not to have love
in your heart.

Do I love things and use people or love people
and use things?

The most I can do for any person is to love him.

Work is love you can see.

I must love you like I love myself.

Sometimes it's your turn and sometimes it's my turn.

Love reminds a friend when he makes a mistakes
if he does not seem to know.

Love your enemies, do good to them that hate you . . .
that you may be children of your Father which is in heaven:
for He makes His sun to shine on the evil and on the good,
and sends rain on the just and unjust.

Love can't be wasted.

Love never fails!

A friend is a present you give yourself.

A friend can seem as close to you as your brother,
sometimes closer.

You can act any old way with your friend,
but you really shouldn't.

Even when I make a fool of myself, my friend still loves me.

Love is patient.

Love is willing to wait.

Love grows.

Love is kind.

Dear God,
Help me do the things I should
To be to others kind and good,
In all I do in work or play—
To grow more loving every day.

Love tells a friend when he gets on the wrong road.

The way I want my friend to treat me is exactly how
I should treat my friend.

Do unto others as though you were the others.

Jesus is my best friend!

If nobody loves me, it is my own fault.

The greatest joy is to love and be loved.

We would love each other better
if we only understood.

We learn to love better as we grow older.

Love is enough.

Life is nothing but a growing in love.

Not what we receive, but what we give
is the essence of Christian love.

We may give without loving, but we cannot love without giving.

The love of God is broader
Than the measure of man's mind;
And the heart of the Eternal
Is most wonderfully kind.

Love is the law of life.

All good gifts around us
Are sent from heaven above;
Then thank the Lord, O thank the Lord
For all His love.

Jesus, what did You find in me
That You have dealt so lovingly?
How great the joy that You have brought
O far exceeding hope or thought.

The end of all learning is to know God, and out of that knowledge to
love and imitate Him.

God only is the Maker
Of all things near and far:
He paints the wayside flower,
He lights the evening star:
The winds and waves obey Him;
By Him the birds are fed:
Much more to us the children,
He gives our daily bread.

JOY

Today, whatever may annoy, the word for me
is joy, just simply joy.

Every day is a good day—some are just better than others.

A Morning Prayer—
Father, I thank You for the night,
and for the pleasant morning light,
For rest and food and loving care,
And all that makes the day so fair.

Rejoice and be glad today!

A Morning Song—
Jesus wants me for a sunbeam
To shine for Him each day—
In every way try to please Him,
At home, at school, at play.

It is more fun to give than to get.

God wants us to be happy.

God made today. I shall be happy today.

God is happy when I pray to Him.

All heaven is happy when I am sorry for my sins
and ask God to forgive me.

God has put this joy in my heart.

The Lord has done great things for us—that's why we are glad.

If I am always feeling sorry for myself, I should be.

If I am lonely, it is because I am building walls
instead of bridges.

We cannot always control what happens around us, but we can
control how we feel about it.

To multiply happiness, divide it.

To make me happy, do not add to my possessions
but subtract from my desires.

Humdrum is not where I live, it is what I am.

Happiness is not getting what you want but wanting what you get.

I could have things I wish for if I didn't spend so much time wishing.

Happiness is not where you are going—
it is a manner of traveling.

The secret of being happy is not to do what you like,
but to like what you do.

He who wants little always has enough.

Nobody can take my joy away from me unless I let them.

God gives me all these beautiful things that I may enjoy them.

Life is like licking honey off a thorn.

Joy on account of or joy in spite of?

When I have thanked the Lord
For every blessing sent
But little time will then remain
For murmur or lament.

Few pleasures are more lasting than reading a good book.

If I learn to forgive others and live with thanksgiving
in my heart and on my lips, happiness will find me—
I will not have to look for it.

By reading, I can exchange a dull hour for a happy hour.

I can have more fun at home than any place.

Joy that isn't shared dies young.

Employ life and you will enjoy life.

Happiness is when we feel close to God.

Sorrow, like rain, makes roses and mud.

When I don't get everything I want, I try to think of the things
I don't get that I don't want.

The main business of life is to enjoy it.

I may be rich and have nothing.

I may be poor and have great riches.

Am I an optimist or a pessimist? Do I call traffic signals go-lights?

To be wronged is nothing unless I continue to remember it.

Better to light one candle than to blame the darkness.

I will never injure my eyesight by looking on the bright side of things.

There is no cosmetic for beauty like happiness.

The place to be happy is here.

The time to be happy is now.

Don't just live and let live, but live and help live.

If you ever find happiness by hunting for it, you will find it as the old woman did her lost glasses, safe on her nose all the time.

Happiness is in our own backyard.

All sunshine makes a desert.

The blue of heaven is larger than the clouds.

Defeat isn't bitter if you don't swallow it.

That load becomes light that is cheerfully borne.

Happiness is increased by others
but does not depend on others.

I can be about as happy as I want to be or as sad.

I may be as happy in a cottage as in a mansion.

Pleasant thoughts make pleasant lives.

It takes both rain and sunshine to make a rainbow.

Joy is not in things, it is in us.

Happiness is a thing to be practiced like a violin.

Manners are the happy way of doing things.

The days that make us happy make us wise.

It is not how much we have, but how much we enjoy
that makes happiness.

Laughter is the outward expression of joy.

I consider my day lost if I have not laughed.

Laughter is the music of the heart.

Joy will escape the narrow confines of the heart.

The happiest person is the one who thinks the most interesting
thoughts and we grow happier as we grow older.

Duty before pleasure and neither before God.

The best remedy for unhappiness is to count our blessings.

Do you forget your troubles as easily as you do
your blessings?

If I could count my blessings I would know the biggest number
in the world.

Be thankful for your food and drink.

Thank God for your family and friends.

The Lord daily loads me with benefits.

The morning looks happy. The evening is happy, too.

Praise God from Whom all blessings flow!

I won't confer with sorrow 'til tomorrow.
Today—joy will have her say.

May I not pass this day in search of some rare and perfect tomorrow.

The cup of life is for him that drinks and not for him that sips.

Acts of love and kindness never die
But in the lives of others multiply.

Rise and shine!

When you feel dog-tired at night, could it be because you
have growled all day?

If you don't enjoy your own company, why inflict yourself
for hours on somebody else?

Isn't life splendid and isn't it great? Let's start being happy—
it's never too late.

For the beauty of the earth,
For the glory of the skies,
for the love which from our birth
Over and around us lies,
For the wonder of each hour
Of the day and of the night,
Hill and vale, and tree and flower,
sun and moon, and stars of light,
Lord of all, To Thee we raise
This our hymn of grateful praise.

If I give, it shall be given to me, good measure, pressed down,
and shaken together and running over.

Sow sparingly, reap sparingly—
Sow bountifully, reap bountifully.

A merry heart makes a cheerful face.

No joy exceeds the joy of forgiveness.

Count your joys instead of your woes,
Count your smiles instead of your tears.
Count your gains instead of your losses.

Discover the great indoors!

Today is the only asset I have.

Today is the most important day of my life.

Concentrate on the doughnut instead of the hole.

Let all those that put their trust in God be happy
for God takes care of them.

Serve the Lord with gladness and sing a happy song.

Take joy with you when you go for a walk.

Spilled on the earth are all the joys of heaven.

I have feet to take me where I'd go,
I have eyes to see the sunset's glow,
I have ears to hear what I would hear,
O God, forgive me when I whine;
I'm blessed indeed—the world is mine.

Dear Lord, keep us from having our lives so full of good things that
we don't have time for the best.

No joy exceeds the joy of forgiving and being forgiven.

Back of the loaf is the snowy flour,
And back of the flour the mill:
And back of the mill is the wheat and the shower,
And the sun, and the Father's will.

The busy have no time for tears.

If my mind is unemployed, my mind is unenjoyed.

Now I'm not braggin', but it's understood—
What I do, I gotta do good.

The biggest reward for a thing well done is to have done it.

Everyone's work is a self-portrait.

Nobody has more time than I.

I will sing to the Lord for He has been good to me.

Teach me, my God and King,
In all things Thee to see;
And what I do in anything,
To do it as for Thee.

If I stop to think, I will have reason to thank.

Be the labor great or small—
Do it well or not at all.

All people smile in the same language.

Unlike most things for which we pray,
A smile we keep when we give it away.

A smile can happen in a flash, but the memory
sometimes lasts forever.

A smile is a curve that can set a lot of thing straight.

The best thing to have up your sleeve
is your funny bone.

There is not enough darkness in the whole wide world to put out
the darkness of one little candle.

Laugh a little—sing a little
As you go your way!
Work a little—play a little,
Do this every day!

Give a little—take a little,
Never mind a frown—
Make your smile a welcomed thing
All around the town!

Laugh a little—love a little,
Skies are always blue!
Every cloud has silver linings,
But it's up to you!

Do we enjoy what another needs more?

What word is made shorter by adding a syllable? Answer: Short.

We cannot have mountains without valleys.

If I try to make others happy, I am happier than they are.

We can even smile through our tears if we try.

Jesus bids us shine,
With a clear, pure light,
Like a little candle
Burning in the night;
In this world of darkness
We must shine,
You in your small corner,
And I in mine.

You can no more hide the inner feeling of true joy
than you can pour the splendor of the noonday sun
into a mold. Joy will escape the narrow confines
of the human heart.

It isn't our position but our disposition
that makes us happy.

PATIENCE

One thing at a time and that done well
is a very good rule—as many can tell.
We can do most anything we want if we stick to it long enough.

I will not fail unless I give up trying.

Failing is not falling, but in failing to rise when you fall.

You may if you try—
You won't if you don't.

The burdens don't matter as long as I remember
to give them to God.

No difficulties, no discovery. No pains, no gain.

The secret of success is hard work.

Education is hard, hard work, but it can be made interesting work.

The grass may seem greener on the other side,
but it is just as hard to mow.

It does one good to be somewhat parched by the heat
and drenched by the rain of life.

To find fault is easy; to do better may be difficult.

If all men are created equal,
it is because they have 24 hours a day.

It is easier to be critical than correct.

Pay to no one evil for evil.

Overcome evil with good.

Be patient with everyone.

Murmur not.

Let us then, be up and doing
With a heart for any fate,
Still achieving, still pursuing,
Learn to labor and to wait.

When you think you are at the end of your rope,
tie a knot in it and hang on!

If we hope for that we see not, then do we with patience
wait for it.

When God makes an oak tree, he takes 20 years. He takes only
two months to make a squash.

Were I chaste as ice and pure as snow, I should not escape slander.

You are only young once, but you can stay immature
almost indefinitely.

When you are through changing, you're through.

Age has many blessings youth cannot understand.

Habit, if not resisted, soon becomes necessity.

One thing at a time and that done well
Is a very good rule—as many can tell.

Anytime a person takes a stand, there'll come a time when he'll be
tested to see how firm his feet are planted.

No one is as old as he hopes to be.

Better let them wonder why you didn't talk than why you did.

Habits are first cobwebs, then cables.

Commit a sin twice, and it will seem no longer a sin.

Habit can be my best friend or my worst enemy.

Is it true? Is it necessary? Will it help?

Use speech for spreading good will.

He who keeps his mouth and his tongue
keeps his soul from troubles.

He that can rule his tongue shall live without strife.

A fool utters all his mind; but a wise man keeps it in till afterwards.

He that has knowledge spares his words.

He that refrains his lips is wise.

In a multitude of words there lacks not sin.

Tact is the ability to close your mouth before someone else wants to.

Best rule I know for talking is the same as the one for carpentering—
Measure twice and saw once.

Some people need a double chin. There's too much work for one.

We weaken what we exaggerate.

Listening is wanting to hear.

When music speaks, all other voices should cease.

Taste your words before you let them pass your teeth.

Do not say a little in many words, but a great deal in a few.

Silence is not always golden—sometimes it is just plain yellow.

Prayer: Set a watch, O Lord, before my mouth; deep the door
of my lips. Let me say the right things rightly.

Let not the sun go down upon your wrath.

The gilding of the key will not make it open the door better.

Dope is for dopes.

Think: Will this turn me on or will it turn on me?

There's a slight difference between keeping your chin up and sticking your neck out, but it's worth knowing.

If I know enough to do a thing, I know enough not to do a thing.

Don't tell your friends about your indigestion: "How are you" is a greeting, not a question.

Prejudice is being down on what we are not up on.

Old-timers who recall the hip-deep snows of their childhood should remember that when they were children their hips were lower.

If you have a weakness, make it work for you as a strength—and if you have a strength, don't abuse it into a weakness.

Somebody thought Anybody would do it,
and Somebody thought Everybody should. Guess who finally did it?
That's right—Nobody.

Everybody's business is nobody's business.

God has a song to teach us, and when we have learned it amid
the shadows of affliction, we can sing it forever.

A man shows what he is by what he does with what he has.

Many of the things that go wrong surprise us by turning out all right.

More people would be on Easy Street if they were willing to go
through a tough neighborhood to get there.

The greatest and most sublime power is often simple patience.

Not so in haste, my heart,
Have faith in God and wait:
Although he lingers very long,
He never comes too late.

God never comes too late,
He knows what is best.
Vex not thyself today in vain,
Until He comes, I rest.

MEEKNESS

Dear Lord, help me never to judge another until I have walked two weeks in his shoes.

Meekness is surrendering to God.

A child may have more real wisdom than a brilliant philosopher who does not know God.

Humble yourself under the mighty Hand of God and He will exalt you in due time.

God resists the proud, but gives grace to the humble.

When I think I stand, I should take heed lest I fall!

Nothing is too small to play a part in God's scheme.

God's strength is made perfect in weakness.

I'd admit my faults, if I had any.

It is no advantage for a man to know much unless he lives
according to what he knows.

A wise son makes a glad father.

Children should hear the instruction of their parents.

The ways of man are before the eyes of the Lord,
and He ponders all his goings.

God gives grace to the lowly.

A meek and quiet spirit is of great price in the sight of God.

Jesus came not to be ministered unto, but to minister,
and to give His life a ransom for many.

In honor prefer one another.

Submit yourself to every ordinance of man for the Lord's sake
for so is the will of God.

If anyone asks you to go a mile, go with him two.

The common people heard Jesus gladly.

A man's life does not consist in the abundance of things
that he possesses.

I brought nothing into this world, and it is certain
I shall carry nothing out.

I am the clay, and God is the potter; and I am the work of His Hand!

Whosoever shall keep the commandments and teach them,
he shall be called great in the kingdom of heaven.

Man shall not live by bread alone, but by every word
that proceeds out of the mouth of God.

Let not the rich man glory in his riches.

Glory only in the Lord.

Every one of us shall give account of himself to God.
Let us not therefore judge one another.

God understands my thoughts afar off and is acquainted with all my
ways. There is not a word in my tongue, but He knows it.

Boast not yourself of tomorrow; for you know not
what a day may bring forth.

I should say, if the Lord will, I shall live, and do this or that,
for I know not what shall be on the morrow.

The Lord is near unto them that are of a broken heart; and saves
such as be of a contrite spirit.

The Lord can mend my broken heart if I give Him all the pieces.

Love not the praise of men more than the praise of God.

Let another man praise me and not my own mouth;
a stranger and not my own lips.

Let not the wise man glory in his wisdom.

God has chosen the foolish things of the world to confound the wise.

Let not the mighty man glory in his might.

God has chosen the weak things of the world
to confound the mighty.

A mighty man is not delivered by much strength.

The dewdrop, as the boundless sea
In God's great plan has part;
And this is all He asks of thee,
Be faithful, where thou art.

Let the little children come unto Jesus: for of such
is the kingdom of heaven!

I can be kind in looks, words and acts.

Every deed of love and kindness done to man is done to God.

True nobility comes of the gentle heart.

The merciful shall obtain mercy.

He that has mercy on the poor, happy is he.

Do you care for the poor at your door?

The Lord is good and ready to forgive; and plenteous in mercy unto
all them who call upon Him.

Be gentle to all people.

The art of being kind is all this world needs.

When we forgive ourselves and others,
God will forgive us.

A non-forgiving heart cannot be forgiven.

Forgiveness is the sweet smell the violet sheds on the heel
that crushed it.

The more perfect we are, the more gentle and quiet we become
toward the defects of others.

Be to his virtues very kind—
Be to his faults a little blind.

Disagree without being disagreeable.

Jesus said that seven times is not enough to forgive. He said
forgive seventy times seven times.

Talk to God as friend to friend.

It takes two to quarrel and it takes two to make up after a quarrel.

I really should be first to say hello—first to smile—
and, if necessary, first to forgive.

If I am stronger than another, I should do more for him
than he does for me.

Has someone drawn a circle and shut you out? You and Love
can outsmart him. Draw a bigger circle and take him in.

It is right that we remember wrongs done to us so that we may
forgive those who wronged us.

It is in pardoning others that God pardons us.

If you are not for yourself, who will be for you?

If you are for yourself alone, then why are you?

Listening is a way of loving.

Maturity is humility. A mature person is able to say, "I was wrong."
He is also able to say, "I am sorry." And when he is proven right,
he does not have to say "I told you so."

A smart alec is a person who thinks he knows as much as I know I do.

Education is the process whereby one goes from cocksure ignorance
to thoughtful uncertainty.

Little drops of water,
Little grains of sand,
Make the mighty ocean
And the pleasant land.

And the little moments,
Humble though they be,
Make the mighty ages
Of eternity.

Don't brag—it isn't the whistle that pulls the train.

A humble, lowly, contrite heart,
Believing, true, and clean,
Which neither life nor death can part
From Him who dwells within.

Meekness is that temper of spirit in which we accept
God's dealing with us as good.

I can see my true significance only after I have realized
my insignificance.

There is no surer sign of perfection than a willingness
to be corrected.

GOODNESS

The smallest good deed is better than the grandest intention.

To every one there opens a high way and a low—
And each person decides the way his soul shall go!

Whatever I sow, that I shall reap.

All things whatsoever I would that others should do to me,
I must do even so to them.

The EYES of the Lord are in every place beholding the evil
and the good.

Even a child is known by his doings, whether his work be pure,
and whether it be right.

Do I practice the behavior I expect from others?

Let us seek not to be better than our neighbors, but better
than ourselves.

Prayer:
Jesus, Friend of little children,
Be a friend to me;
Take my hand and ever keep me
Close to Thee.
Teach me how to grow in goodness
Daily as I grow;
You have been a child,
And surely you must know.

Life is not the wick or the candle—it is the burning.

Resolve to be better for the echo of it.

If anyone speaks evil of you, so live that none will believe it.

We've got to build a better man before we build a better world.

One sinner destroys much good.

If I were faultless I would not be so much annoyed
by the defects of others.

Doing right is no guarantee against misfortune.

Always tell the truth and you won't need a good memory.

Spend so much time on the improvement of yourself
that you have no time to criticize others.

Liberty is not the right to do as we please, but the opportunity
to do what is right.

The earth is full of the goodness of the Lord.

All things bright and beautiful,
All creatures great and small;
All things wise and wonderful,
The Lord God made them all.

Each little flower that opens,
Each little bird that sings,
He made their glowing colors,
He made their tiny wings.

He gave us eyes to see them,
And lips that we might tell
How good is God our Father,
Who does all things well.

God is faithful. While the earth remains, seedtime and harvest, cold
and heat, and summer and winter, and day and night shall not cease.

God is good and He loves us always and in all ways.

Be quiet and think on God's goodness.

Create in me a clean heart, O God; and renew a right spirit
within me, I pray.

Let us bear one another's burdens, and so fulfill the law of Christ.

Feed the hungry, give drink to the thirsty, take into your home
the strangers, clothe the naked, visit the sick and those in prison.
Inasmuch as we do these things unto the least of our brothers,
we do them unto Jesus.

Ever follow that which is good to all men.

Render not evil for evil unto any person.

Be a doer of the word, and not a hearer only, deceiving your own self.

Don't mistake potatoes for principles or peas for piety.

You are not what you think you are, but you are what you think.

Sin is the transgression of the law.

Fools make a mock at sin.

My sins have withheld good things from me.

He who covers his sins shall not prosper: but whoso confesses
and forsakes them shall have mercy.

We don't break God's laws—we break ourselves on them.

Abstain from all appearance of evil.

Honest gain is the only permanent gain.

For when the One great Scorer comes,
To write against your name,
He writes not that you lost or won
but how you played the game.

To be good is fine, but to be proud of it
ruins the whole thing.

A criminal is nothing else but you and me at our weakest, found out.

Would you like to see the most dangerous animal in the world—
the one that can harm you the most? Look in the mirror.

No one can be good to others without being good to himself.

I am asking when I pray "Our Father" to live here
as it is done there.

Pretty is as pretty does.

It shall be well with the righteous: for they shall eat the fruit
of their doing.

It shall be ill to the wicked: for the reward of his hands
shall be given him.

If I am faithful in that which is least, I shall be faithful also in much.

To whom much given, of him much shall be required.

Lying lips are an abomination to the Lord; but they that deal truly
are His delight.

Be holy in all manner of conversation.

The pure in heart shall see God.

If I say I abide in Jesus, I should walk as He walked.

If you talk the talk, baby, walk the walk.

I shall to my own self be true. If I am true to those around me,
I shall be true to myself.

Do the best things in the worst times.

Nobody's perfect, but I'm close.

Sin is not in things, but in the wrong use of things.

If I wish to secure the good of others, I have already secured my own.

Keep your nose clean so you can smell a phony.

The man who lives by himself and for himself is apt to be corrupted
by the company he keeps.

Progress is not changing, but changing for the better.

I am the temple of God and the Spirit of God dwells in me.
I must not defile the temple.

The Spirit Itself bears witness with my spirit,
that I am a child of God.

He who lives to live forever never fears dying.

Live virtuously and you cannot die too soon nor live too long.

Life is a journey, not a home.

Ever follow that which is good to all men.

Blessings are upon the head of the just.

Every virtue we possess;
And every victory won;
And every thought of holiness,
Are God's alone.

Is there anything in the world more spacious
than the room we have for improvement?

Breathe on me, Breath of God,
Fill me with life anew,
That I may love what thou dost love,
And do what thou wouldst do.

INNER PEACE

If we do not find peace in ourselves, it is vain to seek it elsewhere.
Peace is the happy, natural state of a person.

I do my best and leave the outcome to God.

Jesus prays for me!

The Holy Spirit prays for me!

God sees farther than I do.

Be sure your sins will find you out.

No pleasure can quiet my conscience.

Money can't buy a clean conscience—square dealing is the price tag.

Jesus Christ the same yesterday, today and forever!!!!

Any trouble that is too small to take to God in prayer
is too small to worry about.

In times when I am afraid, I will trust in God.

God comforts me like my mother comforts me.

A tiny seed can fill a field with flowers.

When I am still, I know that I am His.

God shall supply all my need according to His riches
in glory by Christ Jesus.

Closer is God than breathing—
Nearer than hands or feet.

We cannot go where God is not.

Freely God has promised, boldly may I ask.

To be a seeker is soon to be a finder.

We get faith by hearing God's Word.

I cannot have a need Jesus cannot supply.

God sends His angels to keep me from harm.

God's eye is on the sparrow, and I know He watches me.

In the great quiet of God my troubles are but the pebbles
on the road. My joys are the everlasting hills.

God gives the very best to those who leave the choice with Him.

God holds everybody in His Hands!

Faith stands leaning on God's Word.

Faith expects nothing from ourselves and everything from God.

Ask, and it shall be given me; seek, and I shall find; knock,
and it shall be opened unto me.

God is able to do much more than we can ask or think.

As the heavens are higher than the earth,
so are God's ways higher than my ways and God's thoughts
are higher than my thoughts.

We pray "God's will be done."

My help comes from the Lord, Who made heaven and earth.

Jesus came to die on a cross of wood
Yet made the hill on which it stood.

God has made the earth, and created man upon it. His Hand
stretched out the heavens, and all their host has He commanded.

Because I have faith I understand that the worlds were framed
by the Word of God and that things which I see
were not made of things which I see.

God said, "Let there be Light" and there was Light!

In Christ are hid all the treasures of wisdom and knowledge.

I am a child of God with the breath He gives me.

There is an outward me and there is an inward me.

Though the outward me will someday perish, the inward me is
renewed day by day.

My body is only my house—it is not the really, really me. That's why
I can be happy no matter what.

Said the robin to the sparrow,
"I should really like to know
Why these anxious human beings
Rush around and worry so."
Said the sparrow to the robin,
"Friend, I think that it must be
That they have no Heavenly Father
Such as cares for you and me."

As my day so shall my strength be.

I can do all things through Christ Who strengthens me.

Take no thought for food or drink or clothes for your heavenly Father
knows you have need of these things.

Seek God first and all these things shall be added unto you.

If I seek the Lord, I shall have a place to live and I shall be fed.

Trust God in every way every day.

Good prayer says "please" and "thank you" at the same time.

A little boy knelt to pray. He said his ABC's but told his mother God
could take the letters and form them into words.

When you pray, don't say, "hello God" and hang up the receiver.
Wait for God to answer. Listen.

Pray for others.

You cannot pray the Lord's Prayer and even once say I—
From the very beginning it never once says me.
Our Father—Give us—Lead us—Deliver us—

A tea party is no fun if there is no one there
but me, myself, and I.

Pray to God for potatoes but remember the hoe.

God is the source of all I need or all I could ever want.

Everything I do is a miracle.

Goodness and mercy shall follow me all the days of life;
and I will dwell in the house of the Lord forever.

Whatever God sends, whether sunshine or rain, it is needed
for that inner me's health.

The ole Devil trembles when he sees me upon my knees.

I love the Lord and all things will work together for good to me.

I walk by faith, not by sight.

If I can see the Invisible, I can do the impossible.

One (and I am one) on God's side is a majority.

No real peace can abide with the man who lives contrary
to the Word of God. In all the storms that beat upon the soul,
one who stands on the promises of God has stability and calm.
In keeping of God's commandments there are great rewards
and peace is only one of them.

To be spiritually minded is life and peace.

Only be still and wait God's leisure
In cheerful hope, with heart content
To take whatever your Father's pleasure,
Knowing it is what Love has sent.

In all your ways acknowledge God, and He shall direct your paths.

With Christ as my Savior, I need neither fear the present
nor be apprehensive of the future. I am safe and secure
in His hands.

God is our refuge and strength, a very present help in trouble.
Therefore will not we fear, though the earth be removed,
and though the mountains be carried
into the midst of the sea.

When you can't sleep, do you count sheep?
No, I talk with the Shepherd.

In heavenly love abiding,
No change my heart shall fear,
And safe is such confiding,
For nothing changes here.
The storm may roar without me,
My heart may low be laid;
But God is round about me,
And can I be dismayed?

No time is lost waiting upon the Lord.

O bless the Lord, my soul!
His mercies bear in mind!
Forget not all His benefits!
The Lord to thee is kind.

Faith is not belief without proof, but trust without reservations.

A grudge is too heavy a load for anyone to bear.

Prayer is so simple. It is like quietly opening a door and stepping into the very presence of God.

Every good gift and every perfect gift is from above, and cometh down from the Father of lights, with whom is no variableness, neither shadow of turning.

The King of love my Shepherd is,
Whose goodness faileth never;
I nothing lack if I am His,
And He is mine forever.

O Lord, may I practice what I preach, and preach what I practice.

Blessed are the peacemakers: for they shall be called the children of God.

Peace I leave with you, my peace I give unto you:
not as the world giveth, give I unto you. Let not your heart be troubled, neither let it be afraid.

Be careful for nothing; but in every thing by prayer and supplication with thanksgiving let your requests be made known unto God. And the peace of God, which passeth all understanding, shall keep your hearts and minds through Christ Jesus.

Wherever He may guide me,
No want shall turn me back;
My Shepherd is beside me,
And nothing can I lack.
His wisdom ever waketh,
His sight is never dim.
He knows the way he taketh,
And I will walk with Him.

Sow a Thought and you reap an Act;
Sow an Act and you reap a Habit;
Sow a Habit and you reap a Character;
Sow a Character and you reap a Destiny.